NONE THE WISER

*How to Create Real Magic in Your Life
and Manifest Your Best 24/7*

David Ian Charnock

10-10-10
Publishing

NONE THE WISER:
How to Create Real Magic in Your Life and Manifest Your Best 24/7
www.nonethewiserbook.com
Copyright © 2022 David Ian Charnock

Paperback ISBN: 979-8-840401-46-0

References to internet websites (URLs) were accurate at the time of writing. Authors and the publishers are not responsible for URLs that may have expired or changed since the manuscript was prepared.

Limits of Liability and Disclaimer of Warranty
The author and publisher shall not be liable for your misuse of the enclosed material. This book is strictly for informational and educational purposes only.

Warning – Disclaimer
The purpose of this book is to educate and entertain. The author and/or publisher do not guarantee that anyone following these techniques, suggestions, tips, ideas, or strategies will become successful. The author and/or publisher shall have neither liability nor responsibility to anyone with respect to any loss or damage caused, or alleged to be caused, directly or indirectly by the information contained in this book.

Publisher
10-10-10 Publishing
Markham, ON   Canada

Printed in Canada and the United States of America

*This book is dedicated to my parents
Ivy Charnock and Arnold Charnock,
to whom I am entirely indebted and,
without their invite to a party back in 1966,
none of this would have been possible.*

*I am me to me,
and
whatever
you
think I am,
I am to you.*

Table of Contents

Acknowledgements

There are so many people I could acknowledge, I would need to write another book. I will therefore limit myself to only a short list, so please don't be offended if you expected to see your name, as you will be in my thoughts always.

Although I remain highly sceptical of our education system, some of the teachers within the system should be awarded a medal for their passion, care, and devotion to duty. It was only during sport that I was truly alive and felt like I was connecting with the real ME.

Mr. Busfield, who managed the Murton Jubilee School football team, believed in me as a footballer and made me captain of the team. He encouraged me and was instrumental in me being selected for the Seaham and District Junior Boys Football Team, even driving me to some of the matches.

The headmaster of Murton Jubilee School was a man called **Mr. Wilson**. He was the best headmaster ever, and I even stood in as part-time secretary for him, answering phone calls while the real secretary was away. When I left Jubilee School and moved to Easington Comprehensive School, it was like moving from a fish bowl into the sea, and I struggled with the enormity of it all. I was so intimidated by the number of children at this school, I decided not to attend the trials for the football team or the selection matches, to whittle down the numbers. One day, my PE teacher, **Mr. Gelson,** called me into his office and asked why I had not attended any football trials for the new team. Apparently, Mr. Wilson had called the school to see if I was captain of the team, and which position I was playing. Stan Gelson put me straight in the team with no trials, and without that call from my headmaster, I'm not sure where I would be today. Thanks to both of you.

When it came to reading books, I started with *Unleash the Giant Within*, by **Anthony Robbins,** which was a fantastic workbook to life and getting on in the world. I remember listening to some tapes by Anthony, and he sometimes talked with too much passion and speed, but it was hard not to be moved by him as a coach.

The next person to touch my life was **Dr. Wayne Dyer,** and I thank him for so many wise books and calming dialogue, which again, like Anthony Robbins, touched my life in so many important, direct, and subliminal ways. Next came **Dr. Deepak Chopra,** who, for me, mixed science with the mind and continues to blow me away with his knowledge and his ability to convey complex information in simplistic terms to the reader. I was fortunate to meet both Dr. Dyer and Dr. Chopra many years ago when they did an event together at the Hammersmith Odeon, London.

There was a time when I decided to join a local Rotary group in my twenties, and on my first visit as a member, I had to give a speech about myself. Not only that, I was told I should make it humorous too. I had never given any sort of speech in public like that before, and I was terrified at the prospect. I had just read a book by **Harvey Mackay**, a top American businessman, and I warmed to his style and was pleasantly surprised to see he was one of America's top public speakers. I therefore wrote a letter to Harvey, and to my surprise, he responded by sending me hardback copies of all his books, and giving me advice on how to conduct a speech for my Rotary event. Thank you, Harvey, and I have always remembered to tell stories in a speech because you will always remember them.

Where would I be without **Robert Kiyosaki** and his *Rich Dad, Poor Dad* book? I actually have all his books and have been very lucky to have met him on a few occasions too. I think Robert was instrumental in opening my eyes to the financial world and how business works, so I am truly grateful.

More recently, I would like to thank **Paul O' Mahony,** who has assisted me more than you can imagine, on all things social media. He is a great guy with a lovely sense of humour and an amazing passion for helping people.

To my friend *Margaret Randall*: She may be surprised to see her name here as we don't see each other often at all, but she is a diamond, and if I ever needed a personal manager, she would be my choice. She is the lady who suggested I go to Las Vegas for a month for an amazing vacation, so I did and never regretted it. She is a first class lady, and her family too.

To my constant companions through a greater part of my life, *David Ross* and *Clive Orton*. I name these two because someone must take the blame for my actions other than just me. Thanks, guys, for being there even when you probably had no idea what I was doing or what I was up to in life.

To my family: To my brother **John Michael Charnock,** who is the leader of the family and took charge of the care of Mum and Dad in their final years, which wouldn't have been easy. To my other brother, **Kevin Charnock,** who introduced me to the Lake District and dislocated my arm as a child, panicking everyone, including me, in the process. Finally, to my only sister, **Karen Charnock,** who opened my eyes to so many things, including magic carpets and self-improvement books.

To the rest of the family too, including their wives and children: **Bill Roche, Anne Charnock, Julie Charnock, Mark Charnock, Danielle**

Charnock, Stephanie Charnock and Paul Charnock. I know my parents were so proud of you all, and that includes my feelings too. I would like to offer a final big thank you to my two brothers and my sister, for simply putting up with me when we all lived at home. It couldn't have been easy having a baby turn up in the house after you were all at junior school age. Patience and understanding is a virtue.

I would finally like to thank Mr. Raymond Aaron, *New York Times* top 10 bestselling author, my personal mentor and coach, and his team for assisting me with my book. They put the WOW back into my world.

There are many more people I could thank, but time, space, and modesty compel me to stop here.

About the Author

Awarded the Authority in Aspiring Entrepreneurs by *New York Times* best-selling author, Raymond Aaron, David has been at the forefront of business development and personal life enhancement across a number of sectors for more than three decades.

The award-winning author currently lives in the UK but travels extensively on his quest to uncover true real magic in people's lives and their businesses, and to reveal the universal tools you have always had at your fingertips to manifest your dreams into reality. David has worked with numerous individuals and businesses combining transformational coaching strategies with a unique approach to life, to help achieve the results his clients dream about and deserve. Whether coaching one to one or in seminars and workshops, David unlocks the secrets of the universe and empowers you to reach out and create a world of real magic for you, your family, and your business.

David's quest began suddenly when he was woken to the grim realisation that he was simply NONE THE WISER about life and business, and distraught and frustrated having received very little education and insight into the true magic of life. David set out on a journey to not only uncover true meaning but to create a universal toolbox of real magic for everyone to use and to ultimately orchestrate and press their very own human reset button. Everyone has time to press their reset button, and David has been instrumental in finding true meaning for his clients and helping businesses to uncover a new formula for greater prosperity and contentment.

With this book, he has shared his awakening of being "none the wiser," and has delivered years of experience, thoughts, guidelines, approaches, and tips that have helped many people and businesses across the world to increase bottom line profitability and to experience more fulfilled lives.

Your exciting and magical journey starts today with David, but that's not the end by any means. David awaits you online to continue your quest into a more fulfilled and abundant lifestyle through his online platform, www.nonethewiserbook.com. Not only does David help businesses and aspiring entrepreneurs to start up, he will coach and support your development, and transform your personal life too, along your pathway to abundance.

Foreword

Have you ever had time to stop and think about your life, and consider whether or not it is what you had planned for yourself? Have you ever thought that you need to find and unleash the real *you* in life, but never knew how? You probably have lots of aspirations and goals in your mind, and often dream of an amazing, abundant life. However, perhaps your life has been hijacked and filled up with obligations and general activities that do not relate to your passions and goals. You may be starting to believe that you are slowly moving away from any hope of attaining an amazing and abundant life for yourself.

For you to transform your life it will take time, passion, courage, and a lot of self-awareness. David Charnock is someone who has awakened from his slumber, and not only transformed his life but has questioned the very meaning of existence. He has connected with the gifts that the universe has to offer. Through this book, he sends you belief and hope that you too can be taught to transform your life in simple but magical ways, enriching your world and manifesting greatness every day. His words unlock something special inside that you may not initially understand, which may be different from what you know, but you will come to understand intuitively that what he is saying is true.

David's quest is simple. He is on a journey to teach and educate you that there is another way to see, feel and live your life. His goal is to help you unlock real magic in your world, and to make your journey a truly extraordinary one.

This book contains stories, tips, and suggestions to transform your existence and start living the life of your dreams. I'm sure you will find many messages in this book that will resonate with you, and which you will be able to implement into your life immediately. Start by digesting and applying the content now, and move toward an irresistible and extraordinary life.

Raymond Aaron
New York Times **Bestselling Author**

Chapter 1

Welcome the Wiser

1

I Was Wise Once

My purpose in writing this book is for you to connect with me today and begin a journey that will allow you to create true real magic in your world, and manifest the future you have always dreamed about. You will create your own real magic, manifest the world that you want, and live a life that not only fulfils you but most importantly allows you to be truly YOU!! Wouldn't it be utterly amazing to enjoy the rest of your life on your terms, becoming the person you were meant to be, living the life you always wanted, and savouring each moment along the way?

So, what is your story so far? I'm sure you have one. I'm sure if you sat down for a few minutes and you had to summarise your life, you could pick out a few incidents that shaped it so far. What about if you also had to describe yourself? Oh wow, how would you describe yourself? Are you enjoying your life so far, and has it been packed full of wonderful moments? Are you the person that you always wanted to be, or are you unhappy with how you see yourself, or maybe how you feel other people may see you? For some people, this is a difficult task to carry out and can be painful and sometimes filled with dread. Let me ask you another question though. Who said that your version of your life and the person that you think you are, is correct? Who created that version? Who validated it for you? Most importantly, does your version serve you anymore, and is it holding you back in life?

It took me 30 years to wake up and realise that I was simply "none the wiser." I had no idea who I really was, what I wanted, and what made me happy. Despite being successful in my career, my life seemed empty and soulless. It took me another 20 years to learn how to create my own personal magic and uncover the life that I had always wanted. My gift to you today is to offer you all those 50 years combined of awakening knowledge compacted into this very book you are holding. Let me allow you to fast track your education in life and, most of all, uncover the hidden magic, which is the ultimate free gift to you from the universe.

I believe that within us all is the divine knowledge of the universe. We unfortunately have lost touch with this universal magic and the powers that it can bestow on us. Your challenge is therefore to reconnect to your source. In this book, I will show you how I went from being "none the wiser" to becoming "simply the wiser," using my own personal experiences and techniques from my coaching practice.

I Accepted All the Gifts

At the time of writing this book, it is the 8th month of dealing with the COVID-19 virus, in the year of 2020. For me, personally, this year was supposed to be a year for travelling, which started off on the island of Tenerife, followed by short breaks in Lisbon and in Amsterdam. In March of this year, COVID-19 started to influence England, which resulted in my break being cut short in Amsterdam, and returning earlier than I expected to the United Kingdom. COVID-19 has resulted in mass alterations in the way we live our lives, and has created new habits and ways of working that would not have been imagined a year previously. How we will come out of this virus remains to be seen; however, there has been nothing in my lifetime that has changed the face of this world so much as this virus has done to the population.

From the moment we are born, our lives are being moulded, shaped, indoctrinated, or however you wish to describe it—we are a sponge for information in all its forms. Even before we are born, from the moment of conception, we are being influenced by Mum and the environment around us while we begin to form and develop. So many times, during coaching sessions, a client will raise an issue in their current life, which was most probably formed in their childhood, or certainly earlier in life.

I will show you how to re-program yourself and to break free from the outdated beliefs you have held onto over many years. Most of the problems we experience in life today, we can resolve. We learn beliefs, habits, and skill sets throughout our lives, but most importantly when we are younger; however, although they may have served us perfectly adequately up until now, we need to update at times. Like a computer, which from time to time needs to have its operating software updated, we are very similar in the process.

All too often, we accept the gifts that were given to us from the day we were born. Opinions, phobias, and beliefs from other people around us become ours and are gratefully accepted until maybe one day we wake up and don't recognise the person looking back at us in the mirror. It's almost like deciding to go out shopping for the day and buying clothing that everyone else desires, and then coming home and unpacking to find you don't like anything you have bought.

When I was a child, I had auburn hair, and although I didn't realise it at the time, Mum had concerns about me standing out from the other children or being picked on and bullied because of the colour of my hair. She also associated auburn or red hair with having the trait of a bad temper, and in addition wouldn't dress me in red clothing or bright clothing either. Those traits became ingrained in my subconscious and were taken forward by me into adult life. As a result, when I was in my twenties, my hair colour had changed from a dull auburn, as it slowly lost its richness, into a light brown colour.

5

Despite the transition of hair colour from auburn to brown, none of my beliefs about who I was and what I could wear had changed at all. I was then a young man with brown hair, who couldn't wear red or bright colours, and had a questionable temper. I had become pigeonholed and was condemned to a life of dull clothing, and was hesitant about expressing myself or showing any anger in any way, at the risk of defaulting into my pre-determined character trait. How many of you have brought some beliefs through from your childhood and are tired of them now holding you back? Raise your arm now and acknowledge this to yourself, and decide that now is the time to change.

I Was a Sponge for Everything

The problem at childhood, and there was nothing that could be done about it at the time, was that we were simply a sponge for everything around us. Everything we touched, looked at, tasted, listened to, and smelled was stored in our computer. But now, like computers, we can change our operating software and memory. That old software that doesn't fit in with the world we see and desire any more, can be a thing of the past, and I'm here to allow you to upgrade at last. How funny it is to say that I could be a 54-year-old male operating on installed software that was first developed in 1966, and have moved forward with very few upgrades over those years, if any.

Name me one piece of technology that you currently have in your possession that is that old and still serves you well. We are lucky if we keep our phones for more than two years without a change or upgrade; however, we seem to feel that it's perfectly acceptable to remain operating on human software that is decades old. Now don't misunderstand me. I'm not saying that everything we consumed and inherited whilst a child is now outdated and superfluous—far from it. If you are happy with your software, far be it for me to say that any changes are required; however, if you have reached a stage in your

6

life when you think it is now time for a change, then let's liberate ourselves and make those changes wholeheartedly.

Let's not become anchored to beliefs or software that don't serve us anymore. Let's confidently accept that we can change ourselves, like how an actor who plays a role in one movie can then pick up a script for another movie and become a different character. Is now the time for you to pick up a new script, to start a new movie, to play a new role, to enter a new YOU world—a world of which you have always wished to enter, and a role which you have always wanted to play? I will show you how to go through your life from now on, playing the characters you want, in the movies that you've always wanted to be in.

How exciting is this going to be for you? How liberating will this be when you learn the skills that will take you forward in a positive way, and develop you into the person that you always wanted to be in life? Imagine how you will feel. Sit for a moment and just take that all in, and imagine how you will feel playing the roles that you were always destined to play in life, never being hindered by those limiting beliefs of the past but only developing empowering beliefs moving forward, and focusing on the goals that you need to focus on to achieve the sort of life that you have dreamed about having always.

I Operated with Too Few Filters

One of the problems we have from early life is that we operate with too few filters. What I mean by that is that we are full of potential and we are a sponge for knowledge; however, what we lack from those early years is the benefit of experience. We take on board this knowledge but invariably do not understand how to use it, and therefore can naively use it in incorrect ways. Take your mind back to when you were a child, maybe a young child, and remember how trusting you were of your parents and how they would look after you.

7

Can you remember a moment when you took that trust outside into the world and found that other people were not the same as your parents, and would not have your best interest at heart?

This was sometimes a shocking revelation. How could people not care for you as much as your parents? However, this was indeed the case, and only experience would mould you to realise that you need to operate with caution when dealing with the people in your life. You are experiencing life every moment, and how you perceive, process, and store those experiences constantly shape and mould you. How wonderful it would be to go back in life and install some filters, filters that would serve you well and encourage empowering beliefs that take you forward in life. Alas, life is not that simple, and I spend many an hour when coaching clients, working on removing limiting beliefs and replacing them with empowering beliefs, similar to an actor putting down one script and picking up a new script to learn. Is it now that time in your life to pick up a new script? If it is, then you are in the right place at the right time, reading the right book.

Hello!!! This is now the time for you to play a new role in life. However, to create the life that you have always wished for, means that you will have to let go of your old life. This will be your only loss in life, having to let go of the old one. However, we have acknowledged that as you go through life, there are times to upgrade, like a computer, and sometimes it is long overdue. So, let's embrace this moment. Imagine if you could never upgrade your software; imagine if you had to deal with technology that was decades old, like using a telephone that was so old and difficult to use, whilst friends were going around using new technology—how would that feel? It's now time to move on, and you have that opportunity available to you. You can dispense with the old filters, which probably served you well for a while but are now unable to take you forward in this world, a world that is ever changing and evolving; you now have an opportunity to grow and evolve with it. So, let's embrace this opportunity 100%.

No Operational Manual

Brace yourself now people, and hold on tight for this part. In February 2002, Donald Rumsfeld, the then US Secretary of State for Defence, stated at a Defence Department briefing:

"There are known knowns. These are things we know that we know. There are known unknowns. That is to say, there are things that we know we don't know. But there are also unknown unknowns. There are things we don't know we don't know."

Now read it again and take it all in. What is Donald really saying here? It sounds like a tongue twister, and it sounds slightly confusing, but read it and think about what he is saying. I know when I first read it, I was none the wiser, but then it got me thinking deeply about my world and myself.

I know there are things that I know ! know. I know I can ride a bicycle; I know that I enjoy coaching people. I know this because I have indeed ridden a bicycle on numerous occasions, and I get pleasure from helping people, so I know coaching is enjoyable for me. But what if I had said that I know I'm ugly or not a nice person. How do I know this? More importantly, is it true?

But Donald also went on to say that there are known unknowns, meaning we know there are things we don't know. We know we will die one day, but we don't know the exact day, of course. We know that we can improve our mind and learn things, but to what level can we raise our capability up to, and what can we achieve? Let me digress now slightly; please indulge me for a moment. So if we know we can do better in life, if we can achieve more, if we can create the life we want, maybe the unknown part is that we simply don't have the key yet to unlock the part that says "this is how you do it?!!" Maybe if we decide to not doubt the "knowing that we can improve this" part, we

9

simply need to find that golden key to unlock the unknown final part to success.

What situation do you currently have right now where you know there is a solution to your problem, but you just haven't found it or unlocked that unknown part of the puzzle yet? This statement therefore gives us hope, doesn't it? From a known, we perhaps uncover an unknown. How exciting could this end up being, I wonder.

Donald's final part was that there are also unknown unknowns— there are things we do not know we don't know. Now keep saying it and thinking about it: WE DON'T KNOW, WE DON'T KNOW. How magical is this then? Are we saying that there are still things to learn and uncover? Things we haven't even contemplated yet, unravelled, understood, acknowledged, or invented yet? We simply don't know we don't know yet. But YET is the magic. YET gets us to reach out into the invisible, to maybe imagine and contemplate something, and then eventually, magically manifest it from the invisible to the visible. IS THIS POSSIBLE? Damn right it is.

Everything you have in your life right now started as a thought— someone's idea that was once unknown and was brought from the invisible world into reality. We all have unknown unknowns, and by exploring our soul, we can create not just a life that will make you happy but a life that you were truly destined to enjoy and uncover. It's waiting for you to wake up and realise that you are no longer "none the wiser."

Where's the Library?

I was brought up and lived my childhood in a village called Murton, in County Durham, England, a very hard-working mining community. At one time, you couldn't visit a mine in the area without being able to see another one in the distance. We lived on the edge of the village and, at the end of the street, there used to be Murton Bridge, which took you off into the countryside and woodland plantation. Once through the woodland, you reached a crossroads in the pathway. Straight ahead directed you to Eppleton Farm via a large cow field, and left would take you to Tattenham Corner on the main road from Murton to Hetton; right would take you to the stone road and then up to the scouts wood.

On this occasion, I decided to walk straight ahead, aiming for Eppleton Farm. Once into the large cow field, I would always see a huge round water trough, into which my first springer spaniel dog, Benji, would always jump, especially on hot summer days (yes, we did have them), much to the displeasure of the cows that had to drink out of it later. I would then walk up the hill towards the farm, but on this particular day, I came off the path and strode into the long green grass. I was halfway up the hill, in the middle of the field, and turned to look at the view. I could see all of Murton and, to the left of the village, I could see Seaham Harbour and the sea.

As I stood in this spot and took in the view, the sun warmed my face, and I decided to lie down in the long grass and stare at the blue sky and the odd, puffy white cloud. It then hit me: I was in my own little world, staring up at the sky, surrounded by long grass and pointing up to the heavens. As my back sunk into the flattened grass, my mind wandered, and I began to wonder what life had in store for me. I was 15, but what was I going to do in life? What would become of me, I wondered? The sky and the moment was wonderful and perfect. I was enjoying a known unknown moment. I knew I was going to have an interesting life, but I had no idea what form it would take.

As I lay there watching the clouds float past, I decided that when the time was right, I WOULD RETURN TO THIS SPOT. I would return to this spot when I knew what my life was all about, and I could return and answer the questions I had when I was 15. I'm not quite ready to return to that spot yet, but when the time is right and I have my answers in my head, I will return to meet that younger person I once was, and flatten the grass once again.

Learn more in the next chapter, about how accepting we are of a boring, limiting existence in life, and how we learn to accept a way of living that is far from the way we could be enjoying our lives, if we only knew what to do to stop it, and how to connect to the real magic.

It's time to start thinking differently. Here are a few questions for you to answer and take into the next chapter.

Questions:

- Have you tried journaling before in your life? It's your life, so it's worth recording, especially if you want to learn, progress, and be the person you truly are and want to be in this lifetime. Record everything that seems important, taking no more than 10 minutes each day. How do you feel first thing in the morning, and why? What do you feel grateful for today (choose at least two things each day)? What are you drawn towards in life? What are you feeling negative about? Record your disappointments, and record your successes. This is all important and will give you a progress path on your journey from A to B.

- What did you look like before you were conceived? Oh wow, I love to start with the tricky questions first. Look, it may sound like a daft question, but have a stab at it. Who is going to say you are wrong? There are no wrong answers.

- What are your earliest memories from when you were a child? What did you laugh at? What did you enjoy doing? What made you excited? What felt right in your life?

- Look at nature around you. Isn't it wonderfully perfect? How much detail has gone into making nature amazing? No corners were cut with nature. You, too, are amazing, but now for the proper question. Who are you? WHO ARE YOU REALLY? Write it down. What roles do you play each day? You may be a mother, father, brother, sister, parent, boss, employee, or a friend or an enemy. All of these are roles you play. You swap from one to the other at a moment's notice, and each one is different. Write down the roles and characters you play, and then ask yourself: Which one is you? Who are you?

Bonus Real Magic Formula:

Some people never wake up to the world of real magic. Something has guided you to this very moment with me, and luckily for you, it did. You are fortunate, but now you must decide what your next step will be. Before making any further progress along your journey, you must start by saying thank you to the universe for waking you up. Your gratitude is required for everything you have in your life today—good, bad, or indifferent—because it has all made you the person you are now. THANK YOU. Be grateful for all you have manifested in your world. What you have today, came from the invisible into the visible world you are currently experiencing. Its magic, and it was all your doing. So be grateful, show gratitude, and appreciate all you have, because if you do this consistently, more will materialise. You are experiencing an abundant universe.

GRATITUDE IS REAL MAGIC

Chapter 2

Mindset Made Up

2

All in Good Faith

I believe that most people are quite passive, generally. What I mean by that is that we generally go with the flow in life. When I meet someone for the first time in a coaching scenario, it's almost like the person I am talking to initially, isn't taking responsibility for their day-to-day life or existence. Generally speaking, they are being carried along or distracted, shall we say, by the daily demands of life. Let me give you an example of what I mean, and see if it resembles anything like your world, either now or in the past.

A typical morning for me used to be awakening to my alarm going off at 6:30 a.m. Now I really needn't have bothered setting an alarm, because I had probably already been awake an hour beforehand. I typically didn't sleep thoroughly at all, with frequent moments of awakening during the night, in cold sweats. Frequent sleepy glances towards my digital clock radio indicated the countdown had begun to the start of a new day. By the time 6:30 a.m. arrived, I was still incredibly tired if not exhausted, damp with moisture from perspiration, and not particularly looking forward to the day.

Although I had taken my body to bed for the night, in an attempt to rest and recharge my depleted batteries, my mind had subcon-sciously remained awake all through this process, focusing on stressful topics and unfinished business. Strange things would also happen frequently during my bedtime sleep patterns. Frequently, I would settle down in bed to rest, with many questions in my head, and quite often I would wake up during the night with the answer, or even remember things I had forgotten to do. Does this resonate with any of you?

I found it a struggle to get out of bed most mornings and would have quite depressing thoughts just before throwing the quilt back to depart my slumber pad. Within 30 minutes, I had brewed and drank my first cup of tea for the day, and given my mind a quick opportunity to calm down and put the chaotic worries I had, into some kind of normality.

My start to the morning was never anything new; in fact, it was quite the opposite. It was all about routine; possibly a comforting routine that made me feel as if this was the correct pattern to follow. Breakfast Television followed the same format, providing me with some person's version of the news they thought I needed to listen to and accept. I always find it amusing how the weather seems to always matter on Breakfast TV, but why? It never ever really mattered to me as I was going to remain generally indoors for the day, working. I suppose glancing out of the window would either be a relief if it were raining, or a tease if the sun were shining brightly; however, the weather forecast was invariably incorrect.

After shower time and getting dressed, I would then be off on the same journey to work, with the same expectations for the day, and the same welcome as I entered work, with the same office gossip and politics taking place. Now let me stop myself right there for the moment. I'm sounding a little depressed, but I wasn't; I'm simply describing a start to the day, a day in our life—omg, my life—which is so like the four other days of the week in which I work. My life has developed into not only a routine but a bunch of habits that has taken over and dressed itself up as my apparent wonderful life. I was simply going through the motions, not really connecting with my day truly or my life. It was like living out the life of someone else, an imposter who had taken my life over and had installed rituals, habits and customs that simply were not me. But who was the ME living this life each day?

Let me stop again. Do I need to go on with this example of a day? Good grief, no; you get the gist, I'm sure of it. Surely, I deserve more out of this world than this, please? When did my true life get removed and this hoax of a life get installed? How did this happen? Well, it didn't happen overnight, let me tell you; and if any part of your life resembles this life, then you have fallen into the Earth hoax, and you need to stop it right now—and yes, you can actually stop it. Don't get me wrong, we all need a little routine, but I actually felt lost, uninspired, stressed, and to be honest, I felt that life was capable of offering me so much more and that I was missing out. The strange thing was that I always felt that I was supposed to just simply accept this kind of life, like I didn't deserve anything better or that I had been groomed by society to accept this without question.

When I coach people, they generally have simply accepted this hoax life naturally, and not only embraced it but have built further layers on top of it, like constructing a building on top of a foundation. Quite worryingly, they have done this all in good faith without knowing quite what they do and the ramifications of these actions. I felt I had lost my way in life, in amongst a mass of boring routines and heavy responsibilities. I was capable of so much more if I could only find the real ME.

They Know Not What They Do

So many of our habits, actions, and thoughts are controlled and appear to be brought about by us as individuals, but is that indeed the case? Are they really our own thoughts, ideas, passions, and goals that we look to implement each day? I wonder. Do you wonder too? Our school system, in my opinion, leaves our pupils ill-equipped to deal with basic life when they leave the education system. It is further governed by your social family background and peer group influences. But what chance do school leavers have in life when they receive little or no financial education?

You will get nowhere in life if you fail to understand finance and how to use money, savings, and investments to your best advantage. Most teenagers have never heard of compound interest, let alone how it works. It's almost as if our education system is primarily educating the next wave of corporate slaves, if you are lucky. If you are unlucky, then you fall into the state funded system, where the best you can hope for is to get an education on how to fill out a claim form to your best advantage and receive government financial support. A few people beat the system and make it big, but the majority of people achieve a level of income and lifestyle that reflects the level of education they have received, and the average income of their peers.

I always remember when I was 15 and my school had a visit from the local careers office. I was excited at the prospect of talking with a professional who could give me information on possible college courses, careers, and how to make the most of any job market opportunities. My meeting with the careers officer was devasting and demoralising. I entered this meeting as a very naive young lad and left it destroyed. I was very sporty and excelled at football, athletics, art, and geography. I told the careers officer that I wanted to be a professional footballer, and if I couldn't do that, I wanted to be a commercial artist.

The officer was a man in a suit who dealt with my career choices with total contempt; he thought the prospect of me becoming a professional sportsman was non-existent. He had no file, information, or school reports on me at all, and he was making decisions for me based on his own view of life and opportunities for a young man coming from an area that was impoverished and working class. He also dismissed the notion of me becoming an artist as a career choice and not as a hobby. I sat in silence. I was simply stunned that despite my apparent talent for sport and art, I was being dismissed and thrown onto the scrap heap.

I felt pointless, talentless, and empty inside. I simply sat there and asked him what jobs I could possibly hope to be offered when I left school, and what industries I could consider. The careers officer had one suggestion and one only. He asked me if I had considered a career in the Armed Forces!! That was it; that was his suggestion. I asked him what the entry requirements were for the Army, and he told me (and this was at that time) that I simply needed to be physically fit (which I was). His only suggestion he had for me was to take a job that had no entry qualifications at all, which almost meant that I had no need to come out of the schooling system with any qualifications.

This meeting took 20 minutes. I was 15 years of age. I had been in the school system since I was 5 years of age—10 years of education, to be told I could only expect to get a job that needed no formal qualifications. It took 20 minutes to destroy my 10 years of education. It was as simple as that to destroy any hopes of an exciting and prosperous life. I found the prospect of joining the Armed Forces abhorrent, and therefore what else could I look forward to in life? NOTHING ... and I was NONE THE WISER yet again.

Blind Faith

It's quite strange really when you look back on your first few years on this planet. Typically, we are brought up by one or two parents. Our first few years as a baby involves us being cared for on a total full-time basis and becoming a sponge for everything we see, hear, touch, taste, and smell. It's a rapid learning curve like no other. There is no other time in your life when you are exposed to so much new data, and this data bombards you from every corner of your existence. Unbelievably, none of this information you receive is vetted or controlled or even approved.

I'm not suggesting a government-controlled education system for toddlers, but I'm simply stating an obvious fact that the quality of your initial education is 100% dependent upon the general knowledge and common sense of the people around you at the beginning of your life. All these free rapid educational modules you receive from people are accepted in blind faith, and the perception is initially that everyone is starting from the same point on a level playing field in this world. How wrong can you be?

As soon as you are old enough to be taken out into the world, you soon realise that things are far from fair, and not everyone is starting from the same standing start. You receive a shocking realisation that others of a similar age have had a very different start than you in life, and already have a similar or different perception of the world. Is now the time for me to start chatting about our perception of things in life and reality? Reality must be a very strange concept. Reality can be very different, for example, if you are colour blind. Same view, however very different colours ... which version of the view is correct? Both? Very possibly.

Perception, therefore, is a version of reality. If your perception of London is that the streets are paved with gold and full of opportunity, then you may visit the capital full of optimism and excitement. How did you acquire that perception? Reality, on visiting, may be completely different. However, if you stopped yourself from visiting the capital because your perception is that there are muggers on every street corner, reality may be somewhat different again, and therefore you could be missing out on a great day in London.

Perceptions and reality can be very confusing and can influence our decision making immensely. In addition, If you had never seen a person ride a bicycle before, and a person brought out these two-wheeled inventions to view, your initial thought, perhaps, would be that you would be unable to ride this contraption. If the person told you how to ride it, then your perception would change somewhat, and maybe you would feel that this could be achieved. It's only when a demonstration takes place of someone riding this invention, that you go from a perception to a stronger belief about your ability to cycle this contraption yourself, because you have witnessed someone else doing so. Ultimately, it's not until you ride this bike yourself, and you go from a belief to a knowing, that you fully accept you can now ride a bicycle.

Some things that we learn in our early years are from the standpoint of a knowing. Other things that we learn are from perception or other people's perceptions, which then influence you. We may get told off as a youngster for misbehaving in some way, but that misbehaving behaviour is only processed as such from the perception of the person witnessing the event. One parent may scold a child for their apparent inappropriate behaviour, while another parent may support and encourage the very same behaviour. All these learning modules are absorbed inside us and are generally accepted in blind faith and never questioned.

Please and You Shall Receive

It doesn't take us too long before we realise that there are rewards for compliance in life, and penalties for disobedience. I'm not sure which year it was or how old I was in fact, but there is a moment in your teenage years when you wake up one morning and realise that Mum and Dad don't always have the right answer or know what is best for you anymore!! Its then that you have a big decision to make. Do you go along with the fact that you know they don't know what they are talking about anymore, and keep quiet, or do you speak out and risk distain?

Risking the wrath of your parents can be quite a disturbing and emotional roller coaster because, basically, you are stuck living at home with them, and they could be capable of making your life a hell. My Mum, when growing up, was basically all about appearances and conduct. "Don't show me up," or "Don't speak until you are spoken to." All these examples inject a massive dose of compliance and prospect of wrath for disobedience, should you choose to go off script. There was also plenty of "Do as I say, not as I do."

I'm smiling as I write this page, as I was regularly quick-witted with "put down" replies to acts of compliance being requested of me by my parents. One particular rude response I gave to Mum was when I was told to stay out of the way when she was holding a "ladies" gathering at our home. Quite often, I was thrown into another room for the evening and banned from leaving it, while Mum and the ladies chatted, drank, ate food, and gossiped till the late hours. I was particularly hungry earlier in the evening and had hinted several times to Mum that I needed something to eat, and these requests had fallen on deaf ears.

Eventually, I built up enough courage to venture out from my room and enter the ladies' arena. My appearance resulted in such stares of shock, you would think I had decided to wear a t-shirt saying, "I'm adopted and proud of it." Mum then broke into a tirade of boastful claims about me, and how she had produced a wonderful son, which I would have gone along with gladly had I eaten in the last 24 hours. Apparently, I was "so intelligent" and got all of my brains from her, she said!!! Unfortunately, my quick-witted rudeness did not prevent me from replying, "Yes, you are right; I must have took all of the brains from you and left you with nothing!!!"

OMG, the room fell silent, which gave me the opportunity to quickly grab a plate of sausage rolls and run for my cell door, otherwise known as the lounge!! I smile widely as I write this, but at the time, my comment went down as a massive insult, as you can imagine, and

I had to lay low for a few weeks after that one. It is similar at school in terms of compliance, acceptance, and receiving accolades. I remember being particularly sporty at school and being a part of the football team for many years whilst I was at a comprehensive. Unfortunately, one year, I chose to run well in the PE session at cross country, and before I knew it, I was being entered into 15,000m, 800m, and cross-country competitions.

I wasn't ready for all the attention and spotlight to be on just me. I was surprised by the attention and, in fact, I hated it. Being on the school football team was fine as there were 10 other boys to share the experience and responsibility. Running was an individual sport, and the spotlight, GOOD or BAD, was on you. After objecting to being selected and told to run in several athletic competitions, I was making myself ill from the pressure and stress, and I bailed out and refused to take part.

At this point, my school life changed overnight. I was immediately dropped from the school football team and told I wasn't welcome to take part anymore, after being continually selected for the team for 3 years previously. The PE teacher who had dropped me, also took me for English Language and made my life hell in the classroom. At 15 years of age, I wasn't ready for the structure of my life to be played around with in this manner. It was an eye opener as to how your life could be made miserable when you don't comply to other people's wishes. Or was it a teaching module on how to do as you are told?

Conditional Fun

Most of life comes with conditions, right? Or outcomes? Can you stay detached from the outcomes? Do you want to? Are you looking to achieve certain targets? Does it relate specifically to pain and suffering, or ideally pleasure? Most of my coaching clients want specific outcomes in their life, and they want it pleasurable. All too often, people have let life pass them by, have unfulfilled lives, or are suffering pain and frustration from earlier choices they had made in their lives, or had not made. As I said previously, I always wanted to be a professional footballer or an artist. The careers officer put paid to that by destroying any possibility of such careers, in a thirty-minute meeting.

All it took was thirty minutes to change my life completely, for the worse. On a positive, if it took only thirty minutes to destroy my life, maybe it would take only thirty minutes again to put it right. Nope, alas not; it took 30 years to put it right. But maybe with the right support circle around you, your life could be put back on track in a smaller amount of time. The problem was that I accepted someone else's view of my prospective life and career. I allowed a careers officer, who had never met me before, to make sweeping judgements on my mindset, passions, and capabilities.

How often do we allow someone, who doesn't know us, to pass judgements about us, and then we take on ownership of them, allowing these opinions to shape our lives for years? Why do we do this? Why do you do this? Is it time to take back ownership of your life? We must become more robust. But how do we do that, and how can we prevent other people from penetrating our defence systems, kidnapping our direction in life, and indoctrinating our minds with their unsubstantiated views about us? How empowering and liberating would it be to take responsibility for your life and decide on what's right for you moving forward? It's now time to talk to your three closest friends, who you possibly trust to give you an honest answer to a question.

Ask them why they like you, what is one strength and one weakness they think you have, and what they would change about you if it was possible. The chances are they will all come up with slightly different answers. So, who is right about you? Try answering the questions about yourself too, before you try this exercise on your friends, and see if they come close to your answers about yourself. Opinion is not fact, is it? Perception is not concrete facts either, is it? And what if it was? Surely, it could only take 30 minutes to change your views, couldn't it? What moulds, shapes, and determines our views, feelings, beliefs, opinions, and perceptions?

If we could determine the answers to these questions, then surely we could use that knowledge to focus on working towards what we really want in life. But what do we want in life, and do we really want it? Is what we want what *we* want, or is it what someone else thinks we should have in life? How on Earth do we find out what we want in life? How do we develop goals in life, and how do we ensure we achieve them? How often do you set yourself a New Year's resolution, and after only a few days let it slip, and then after a week, you have forgotten you ever had a resolution? Crazy, isn't it? Maybe goals aren't the way forward then. We get told to set them, but maybe it's simply our downfall as we set ourselves up to fail. So, what is the answer to get what we really want in life? Now we can get excited.

No Pain, No Gain

So, if goals aren't the total answer, then what is? Well, we will get to that in just a moment. All too often, coaches will go through goal setting exercises with their clients, which could be over 2, 3, and 5 years, or longer, for example. Once you break your goals down into years, months, and weeks, you can apparently make them achievable and slowly work your way to success. So why don't most people reach their goals if it's that easy? What is the real problem about not reaching our desires, and what can be done about it? Sometimes the excuse for failure is that maybe your goals weren't exciting enough for you, and your motivation therefore was lacking. Or maybe you just weren't prepared to sacrifice what was necessary to achieve your goals, otherwise known as "no pain, no gain."

We are encouraged to dream big when goal setting. Imagine that money is no option. Imagine you could do anything without any restrictions. The problem as I see it with this initial goal setting approach, is that by dreaming huge, you end up going way beyond your comfort zone and reality of what you think you can achieve in life. Now this is good in many respects, right? Because it removes the barriers to achieving what you really want in life. The problem is that your route to achieving your goals, although broken down into years, months, and weeks, fails to adapt to your existing life, and transcend it across structurally into your new and proposed world.

What are we talking about here then? Habits!! Our habits, our life—the life we currently have is ill equipped to deal with the new goals we have set ourselves, and therefore we are destined to fail and the clock is ticking. Frustration and despondency results from our inability to change the way we operate our life to accommodate change. Let me give a small but massive example of how you can begin to change your life and create a new outlook and mindset, and ultimately create new habits, cementing the road to your important goals.

I wanted to feel successful and prosperous. I really wanted to FEEL IT. I was driving a four-year-old Ford Focus car at the time, and the colour was burgundy. It was hardly a Ferrari, and hardly showing that I had arrived in a world of opulence. At the time, I had always wanted a silver Mercedes car, with the funny emblem sticking up on the bonnet. MY DREAM CAR!! So, I decided to have one. I converted my Ford Focus into a Mercedes in 5 minutes, without notifying DVLC or Ford Motor Company.

From the moment I sat behind the wheel of my car, I took on the ownership of a silver Mercedes. That was the car I was driving from now on, and the mindset change that came with it stepped me up from being a Ford Focus driver to a top executive Merc driver. But it also came with all the luxury trimmings that I perceived a Mercedes owner to have in life, and I immediately stepped into this new world. I was in receipt of a new life script, and it came will all the mindset changes and new habits that were required instantly and without any hassle. The "magic" was happening.

So please note that setting goals on their own are not enough to be able to achieve them. They give no route from your existing life to your new exciting and much improved life. It's simply a wish list, and you are wishing it to happen. Wishes will not change your life, but new habits will.

NEW GOALS + NEW MINDSET + NEW HABITS = NEW LIFE (NEW LIFE NOW)

In the next chapter, you will realise how amazingly talented you really are and how you can easily re-focus and change your life for good, and not only change your life but keep changing it and evolving as you travel along your path to greatness.

Questions:

- Are you stuck in a blind rut each day? Are you repeating the same things, thinking the same things each day? Write down in your journal some of your daily rituals and thought processes you have each day. Is there a pattern to your tasks and thoughts? Maybe they are Monday to Friday, and then on the weekend you act and think differently? It's good to know how you think, process, carry out tasks, and create habits, daily achievements, and frustrations.

- Think back to the time when you first aspired in life; maybe you wanted to be a ballet dancer or maybe a doctor. How did that feel, and why did you want to be that person or have that job? Had you seen something inspirational as a child, on the TV or on social media? What was the response when you disclosed your passions to another person, parents, or family member? All too often, children's initial passions are not taken seriously and are either ridiculed or ignored. Very few are encouraged and supported to explore further at this vital time in their lives. What passions did you have then, and where are they now?

- Children have quite different starts in life. Once in the school system, different children's lives and environments can shine through into everyday existence. When very young children play together uninhibited, it's almost like they are enjoying a total level playing field together, but once school is under way, the child's home environment and support system/influences, both financial and social, starts to show through more obviously. Did this affect you? Were you told not to socialise with certain people? Were you an outcast and didn't fit in with your social circle of friends? Were you not one of the clever children? How did this make you feel? Did you then start to change the way you thought and felt about people and situations? Did this shape your early life positively or detrimentally?

- Do as I say, not as I do? How often did this show up in your life by people? Can you remember a few instances when this happened, and how did it make you feel? Were you confused and frustrated, or did you find it amusing? Mixed messages can be very counter-productive to children and adults. Were these situations totally unrealistic and simply well-meaning but not fit for everyday life or reality?

- Other people's opinions of us can be so important. We put so much pressure on ourselves to seek out favour and acceptance. How do you feel when you are criticised? We know we don't like it, but how do you react? Do you avoid criticism by seeking favour at all costs and changing your behaviour and opinions? What would happen if you decided to be just YOU and said everything that you truly felt, without being cruel of course, but just being genuine and true to yourself?

- So, what are your habits? What do you regularly do or say, both positively and negatively? How do you decide what habits you will develop? How do you get rid of bad habits? Want to achieve your GOALS? Change your habits, reach your goals. It's that simple, isn't it?

Bonus Real Magic Formula:

When you count your blessings and start to show gratitude for everything showing up in your world, your world starts to change for the better. Magical things, opportunities, people, and events start to turn up in your world, but you must have faith and believe in REAL MAGIC. What you focus on and think about, you attract and manifest into your life. The magic of manifesting is at your fingertips. You have been educated and indoctrinated not to believe but instead to obey and do as you are told. Having faith in manifesting will create a world of abundance and ultimately create your dreams into existence.

FAITH IN THE POWER OF MANIFESTING CREATES REAL MAGIC

Chapter 3

Unravelling the Code

3

It Happened One morning – Whoosh Gone

Unravelling the code is all about having the correct mindset and habits. Just like I imagined I was driving a Mercedes when it was a Ford Focus, the mind can create a new lifestyle as easily as it is for an actor when reading the script in a movie. I had the pleasure of seeing Joanna Lumley, the star of the popular TV show in the UK, *Absolutely Fabulous*. She was asked how she stayed so young looking and with a positive mental attitude. Her response was that everyone suffers from highs and lows in life, but she stayed focused by using her skills as an actor, similar to when she would learn a script and play a certain role.

We all play several roles each day, whether we are aware of it or not. When you chat with your parents, you may very well be playing the role of a son or a daughter. We play the role of a friend and an employee, a husband, a wife, and a neighbour. There are so many roles we play each day; we underestimate how talented we really are and the level of skills we possess. So which roles are we destined to play if you continue as you are currently in life? Which roles are you desperate to try and play in the future? Which ones do you need to rehearse and research to play the part to the level of an Oscar award? Well, I may be getting carried away with the Oscar, but do you see what I'm trying to convey?

We have some roles that we end up playing, which simply don't serve us anymore, but we keep playing them. How about the role of a victim?!!! Oh, wow, now that got some of you uncomfortable reading the word "victim." Quite powerful, eh? But who says you need to play that role anymore? You may play it well, but those parts may not serve you well anymore, and now it's time to look at alternative roles. Yes, you may need to research and rehearse. When Anthony Hopkins, the famous Hollywood actor, was preparing to play the part of Adolf Hitler, he became Adolf in his own home and his everyday life. He would walk around his home and take on the persona and gestures of Adolf Hitler. As bizarre as this may sound, he was creating new habits and practising a new skill set necessary to play a role, the role of Adolf Hitler.

Now I'm not suggesting that you want to play one of the most infamous characters the world has ever seen, but you see the power of what I am saying to you. You are not a tree; you aren't stuck in one place and can only remain fixed to the spot. You can be so creative in your own life and be what you want to be, but you simply haven't been shown how to do it, and neither have you been encouraged and given the skill set to achieve all you desire in life. You have been shown only the very basics of what you can achieve in your life, and you need to realise that NOW!! Honestly, you need to stand up where you are right now and shout, "I AM ME!" In fact, you need to email me right now and tell me you NOW realise you are a free individual and can achieve anything you now want to in life. EMAIL ME NOW.

Even if you still have doubts, even if you need many more tools and particular skill sets to find out what direction you need to go in life, just let me know you hear me, because I care about your new journey in life. By the way, check out my website and my email address; it's just a few button presses away for you to get in touch. You are who you say you are and who you want to be. This is no dress rehearsal; this is your life, and there are no limits to what you can achieve. People have maybe held you back through their comments, but these are just opinions; they aren't factual or possibly correct. Just like an actor who receives reviews after a performance, it is simply

OPINION, and you need to stay detached from the good opinion of others, as Dr. Wayne Dyer would say.

I Didn't Realise This Was It

From the first day I entered the school system when I was five years old, I had been practically told what to do. Everything you did was controlled, and you basically did as you were told. I remember my first preliminary day at the infants school. Children were allowed to go into a classroom to meet the teacher who would be taking them for their first year of education. Mum took me into school that day, and I seem to remember being left for an hour to break the parental apron string and mix with other children. You were allowed to look behind a cupboard curtain and choose a toy to play with, and as my father worked on the buses, I grabbed a big red London bus. It was scary, but the big red bus took my mind off things, and I found it fun to be there.

Unfortunately, the fun only lasted for that day, and joining school was just confusing and conformist in my young mind. Everything was regimental, and thinking was simply removed from the agenda, and you were there to do as you were told. I remember being taught religious educational stories. I found this totally bizarre—TOTALLY. I had been told about Santa Claus previously by Mum and Dad, and the thought of some cuddly, kind man turning up at your house once a year with presents totally appealed to me. I was always puzzled why a man with a white beard, who was being so generous, was made to climb down a chimney to leave gifts, and not be allowed to use the front door!!

Religious education, or RE as we called it, for the next 11 years seemed to be even more fanciful than Santa Clause's annual exploits. A pregnant lady with no place to give birth, being tracked by three wise men; a burning bush; a man coming back to life and rolling a massive stone back from a cave entrance, walking on water, and feeding thousands—it just sounded crazy to me and, most of all, unreal. You were just expected to accept stories and direction from the teachers, and as schooling progressed, it seemed to get even more strict and controlling. You were expected to simply comply.

It was also all about learning new habits—lots of new habits—and there was no room for questioning what was being taught, and I can't remember the content or style ever being questioned. Nothing seemed more liberating than when it was break time and you could go out onto the playground and let yourself GO. And boy, did I let myself go. Playtime was everything to me because then I had the freedom to be myself, to have fun and play games. You would be totally free and left to your own devices until a teacher blew the first whistle.

When the first whistle was blown, then according to the rules, you had to stop what you were doing and stand motionless immediately upon hearing it screech. The second whistle resulted in you walking calmly to line up in your classroom rows, ready to go back to the classroom. My world, as it developed, was certainly one destined for outside the classroom. My life was formed and forged on the school playgrounds of County Durham. I thank goodness for playgrounds, for providing me with MY SPACE in the government's education system. Don't dare blow two whistles in ear shot of me; otherwise, you may witness a rather strange reaction.

80/20 Fun Rule Gone Wrong

So, I believe we have now established that goals, although important, don't always get you to where you need to be, right? Be under no illusions; goals are important and necessary, but they don't always get you from A to B, right? You may dream and have a goal about winning the lottery, but let's face it; to win the lottery, you need to first buy a ticket, and probably several of them unless you are amazingly lucky. So perhaps a new habit of buying lottery tickets may assist you with this goal. Okay, it's an extremely basic example but a true accurate example, if you please. Which brings me to a big point that is so important that it is just as vital as goals and creating new habits.

It's about where you spend your time. Well, to be clear, it's about stacking the opportunities to create good habits and achieve your goals in your favour. To do this, you must manage your time. If you don't manage your time, then your time will manage you, and you will give it away free of charge with no return on your investment. So, you must manage and invest in your time. You only get one moment at a time, and that moment will never be repeated. So, time is important, and therefore you must spend it wisely and create as many opportunities that you possibly can to implement new habits that take you towards your goals in an organised manner. The 80/20 rule will assist you with your quest, otherwise known as the Pareto principle, which states that roughly 80% of consequences come from 20% of the causes.

So, let's use this example and analyse your sales figures at work. Is it possible that 80% of your income originates from 20% of your clients? Maybe 20% of your productive time gives you 80% of your quality ideas? If that is the case, then imagine what improvement you could make if your 20% productive time increased to 30%. Are you getting bogged down with too much paperwork, and you aren't concentrating on looking after your top clients as much as you should? We generally don't value our time as much as we should. So, in an 8-hour working day, using this 80/20 formula, then only 1.6 hours of your day is productive, and the rest is simply lost in low priority tasks. Does this make sense?

So, if you think this is the case for you, then it's time your mindset and focus changed, ensuring more productive time is created by you, and the time wasting is reduced or cut out of your daily life. Once you work out how productive you are, or perhaps non-productive, then it's important to establish where your energy/inspirational highs and lows are in the day. Maybe you are a morning person, or you enjoy late afternoon working sessions. The key is to spend time doing the tasks you need to do, creating the habits you need at the right times of the day, when you are at your peak to work confidently and professionally towards your goals. SIMPLE? You bet your life it's simple, and it couldn't be easier if you tried.

The initial key is to write down, for 5 days, from Monday to Friday, all the tasks you perform during the day. Then highlight those tasks that are most productive and that take you towards your goals and creating new, positive, life-changing habits. You must be accurate with your record taking, and then honest about your productivity. If you are like the way I used to be—I used to struggle to achieve 10% output from 90% input, because I was ill focused and allowed myself to get swamped by pointless tasks and distractions—it's time to be ruthless; you have a mission to conquer your life and make it amazing. If you keep doing the same things as you always have done, then you will keep receiving the same results, if you are lucky. There's no luck in my methods; it's down to mindset, focus, and new habits to get you from A to B successfully.

Who Has All the Answers?

I think that one of the realisations that hit me when I came out of the schooling system, was how alone and unstructured I became overnight. I had approximately 11 years of structured indoctrination, and no one prepared me for school leaving. No one prepared me for life outside the education system. An education system that doesn't prepare you for life, quickly became apparent, and it hit me hard and shocked me to the core. Suddenly, REAL LIFE hit me right in the face with a mighty whack!! I had been taken right outside my comfort zone, and I had no further points of reference to assist me with my next choices in life. I had no one to refer to anymore for advice.

In addition, you find yourself entering a rebellious period in your teenage years, where not only do you realise that your parents don't have all the answers, but you also realise that you need to find some answers and have opinions on life and life's situations. Similarly, when you pass your driving test, you perceive that you are a DRIVER, which indeed you are, but you are a driver with no experience. Well, leaving school was similar. You had been through the schooling system; you had your 11 years of what the state had to offer, and you were given a door to go through, into the rest of your life. You were 16 and with no experience whatsoever. The day you drive for the first time without anyone in the car to tell you which direction to go and what to do, is scary. I remember driving for the first time solo and avoiding having to make any turns in the road that took me across the flow of traffic, requiring me to give way and judge the speed of other vehicles ... it was so scary.

Life is remarkably like passing your driving test, and that's why, when you pass your test, you are so euphoric when you are free to take off on the open highway. However, when you take driving lessons, you are given the Highway Code to follow, the rulebook to driving in the UK. Even that code doesn't fully prepare you with any experience in driving, once having passed your test. Life is therefore even more daunting. No guidebook is provided in life. You rely on your school education, your parents, family, and peer groups for your start in life, and that's where it starts. You will mirror most of what you have available to you, from those people around you in your zone of influence.

The zone of influence shapes your initial start in life, and either gets you off to a great start or holds you back to such a degree that you spend the next 30 years trying to learn and experience what you should have—or should I say, could have—received a lot earlier. This, in a nutshell, is your first 16 to 18 years on this Earth. People who appear to get ahead in life and seem to accelerate are exposed to a different education, an education you couldn't access and benefit from. It may have been a second opinion, a heads up, a direction in life, a connection, a reference, an insight, or a schooling that your zone of influence were able to give you and assist you with that propelled you forward in life.

Do you see how vulnerable this can make you? Or how beneficial this can make you? When you analyse your zone of influence, and I suggest you do so, you need to write a list of all those people around you who contributed to your start in life. This will then show you how you were or weren't influenced, in a good, bad, or indifferent way. The only entity that was possibly structured and could be relied upon for clear, helpful, and necessary life skills, would be your school education. Therefore, school needs to be fit for purpose, which I don't believe it is, or probably ever was for you, and certainly wasn't for me.

Maybe if you went to a private school that was particularly chosen for you, to give you the correct life start that was required, things would be remarkably different. The state education system provides you with an education that the state wanted you to achieve. I will let you come up with your opinion on whether it provided you with the skill set that it should have provided, and could have provided—and if it didn't, then why didn't it?

The Mould Is Broken

We won't dwell too much on why you are currently the way you are, because that is for another time, my friend. This is about you waking up and focusing on your potential and what your true heart desires, and the real passions that drive you and make you tick. It's all been supressed and disguised within you, lost so that you operate to a different agenda. But not anymore; this is your time, and you are slowly waking up to the new you—a you that you have craved to make a return to—to allow yourself to live in a way that was always destined for you. All I would say about your status is that your current mould has now been broken, smashed, and is unable to be repaired, and even if it could be, why would you? You have now had a brief glimpse into your true nature and potential, with a new view of yourself that is simply AWESOME, and you can't wait to come to the surface again and beyond.

In the Bible, it says that when we believe in Jesus, we will do greater works than he did (John 14:12). I would class myself as spiritual, not religious; however, the Bible packs a wonderful punch when it claims what you can achieve. In most people's opinions, Jesus is one of the most significant figures ever to have walked this Earth. For him to claim in his teachings that by believing in him, greater work can be achieved, is something worth noting and remembering. You are in good company; you have amazing potential to achieve much more than you currently know. Take notice of who you are now, and build from it; it may be a firm foundation that will allow you to do so, but even if it needs a new base from which to build, you have the skill set to achieve this NOW.

If you were to spend five minutes and assess where you currently are in this world, you could do no better task than to write down in your notes your top 100 successes. Yes, you heard me, your 100 successes. If you don't think you have had 100 successes, then you definitely need to do this task. You will be able to write down approximately 20 without much effort. But then it may get a little harder. You may start off with exam results, graduation, passing your driving test, getting married, landing a terrific job, earning a salary that you had always wanted, buying a home, a car ... the list is endless. These are all your successes, things to be grateful for, and things you may have taken for granted.

Do your list; the more you write down and the more you think about it, the easier it will get, and believe me, once you get into the flow, you will smash 100 successes. Things you forgot were even a success, things you didn't think were successes but were positive events—write them down, because today you have broken the old mould, and the new you is going to be formed, and I can't wait to chat some more with you and see you further develop your mindset and ultimately develop new habits that will take you forward and make you blossom. But please note, this is not about just tweaking the old you; this is about taking you from being "none the wiser" about yourself, to opening a door into a magical world that will not only amaze you but will transform you and the people around you in your zone of influence.

Am I Fit for Purpose?

Are you therefore fit for purpose? Fit enough? And for what purpose? I suppose the question needs to be, what is your purpose in life? Do you have a purpose? Do you need a purpose? What gets you up in the morning, apart from an alarm? What satisfies you when you climb into bed at the end of the day, rest your head on the pillow, and take a wonderful deep breath and sigh ... what are you thinking at that moment? It's been a good day, and you're happy; or was it a stressful day, and you are unhappy? Who determines whether you have a good day or not? Lots of questions, I know. I apologise, but it's to get your creative thought juices flowing with why and what you are doing each day of your life. Honestly, ask yourself: What am I doing in my life? I'm doing it for a reason, right? I must be doing it for a reason, so what is that reason? Is it just simply to SURVIVE each day?

Or are you on a creative path already? Do you have responsibilities? Have you chosen a path to walk down already, or are you in line for something and are still waiting? Which is it? You must surely know what and why you are doing things each day, don't you? Or are you not so sure? Are you now thinking that you're not aware of why you have ended up here, with these things and people around you? Maybe you are content, and your plan in life has been reasonably productive and quite enjoyable, but now you are a little frustrated, or maybe you are losing your way a little. There is no right or wrong answer. Maybe you are living the dream and you want to live it more? Great stuff; you are still with me and reading, so together we have a chance to receive more magic, or maybe even experience it for the first time.

All too often, people go through their life not thinking. They think they are thinking, but in reality, this is not the case. When I have life-coaching clients, most people are stuck in a rut. They have basically done everything that has been asked of them by society and their zone of influence. They have copied and mirror imaged most of what was around them and what they were taught by everyone they have ever known. There comes a day in most people's lives when they question everything in their lives. Sometimes it's called a midlife crisis, but whatever you call it, it's something that pings inside your head one day, and some people attempt to answer the question they are asked by their subconscious: AM I HAPPY? IS THIS THE BEST I CAN EXPECT? CAN I DO MORE? DO I HAVE TIME TO CHANGE THINGS? WHAT WILL PEOPLE SAY? DO I NEED A NEW JOB? DO I NEED TO GET A DIVORCE? Or general questions to this extent.

When these questions come knocking at the door, most people sweep them under the carpet. It's not until we start to suffer discomfort or pain in our lives that we decide to consider doing something about it. That discomfort period can sometimes take days, weeks, months, or years, but the questions will come knocking, and you will have to decide what your next step is, I'm afraid. You are not alone when this happens. This happens to most people, but how you react at this moment is down to you. Sometimes responsibility can get in the way: "I have two children, a large mortgage, a stressful job, and a loving husband, but I'm not happy with my life." These are big

45

questions that don't always get immediate answers, and nor should they, as you weren't born with a crystal ball, and neither is the magic wand shop located around the corner.

This is the time for you to take a big breath in, hold it for 15 seconds, and then let it out slowly ... always remember to let it out, lol. Relax into your seat and, most of all, don't panic at all. You are in good hands, and you are not expected to have all of the answers now, are you? This is the time when you collect your thoughts, write down a few notes about your life and how you are feeling, and then CONTACT ME. The great thing to remember is that you REMEMBERED! You remembered to wake up in life. That's the hard part over, and you've done it. Give yourself a big cheer and a round of applause. YES, DO IT NOW!!

In the next chapter, you will learn that goals aren't all they are cracked up to be if you don't create new habits for yourself, and what you think about and focus on is pivotal to your magical success in life, plus lots, lots more.

Questions:

- So, write down a list of your daily, weekly, monthly, and annual thoughts and habits. This may seem tricky, but start with annual first. This may include New Year's resolutions, holidays at certain times, birthdays, etc. But start to include how you feel too. Are there mood and feeling habits that occur annually that you have never thought about before? Do you get sad at festive breaks or certain birthdays of departed loved ones? Are you a summer person? Do your energy levels drop at certain dark, cold times of the year? You need to know how you tick before you can change it, right? Weekly habits may include dreading a return to work and feeling horrible on Sunday evenings. Remember that you can change all of this, but let's acknowledge it first.

- I want an exhaustive list of all the roles you play in life. You will be amazed at how talented you really are—mum, sister, wife, husband, employee, brother, friend, football team captain, lover, gardener, etc.—how do you do this? How did you learn all these different roles?

- Where do you spend your time each day? How organised are you, and how do you decide what to do each day? What percentage of your time each day is spent focusing on and achieving your tasks and goals each day? How much of your time is devoted to pointless tasks that simply show up each day, and you willingly accept them and waste your valuable moments? How much more effective could you be if you were organised?

- Are you fit for purpose? You have a CV, right? If you have ever gone for a job interview, you had to write down things about yourself, such as qualifications, experience, and talents, etc. Of course, you have, but have you ever done a CV for your life? What's the difference, I hear you say? Get a piece of paper and draw a line down the middle, and on the right-hand side, scribble all of your goals and aspirations, listing as many as possible. Now, on the left-hand side, I want you to list all of your qualifications, passions, talents, and interests, and don't leave anything out—think hard. Now imagine this was an interview and there was a job available (your goals), and then we have you (your passions, qualifications, etc.) applying for the position. Would you get the job, or would you even get an interview? If not, why not? Are you missing vital passion or interest? This is the GAP you need to bridge to get to your goals. Go do it now and see what's missing, or are you there and ready to go with all the talent and passion you need?

Bonus Real Magic Formula:

When you take responsibility for your world and your outlook, and you believe in what you feel, you can achieve changes. When you change the way you look at things, the things you look at change. When you take charge of your life and body, you then have control of the vehicle that you will use on your journey. The power of the breath and meditation will assist you to connect with the universal invisible force, and allow you to settle, clear your mind, and focus on the things you desire. Your to-do list, or if you like, your true desires in life, are hidden in the invisible world. Allow the magic of the breath to connect you with this world.

THE AIR YOU BREATHE IS REAL MAGIC.

Chapter 4

Baptism of Fire
– I Had No Idea

4

Is This Education or Conditioning?

As I said before, we think we think each day, but if you look at what you do at work and in life every day, you are basically repeating 80% of your thoughts and actions all the time. It's amazing we ever get anything done, isn't it? Or maybe that's why we don't achieve the level of accomplishment that we could if we simply broke free from the social herd. If you watch a flock of sheep, then you will see what I mean. When one gets nervous and shoots off in a particular direction, then most of the others will follow. You very rarely get a sheep who does their own thing regardless of what the herd is doing. They simply don't think, and instead just follow the others whether it is the right thing to do or not. They simply haven't been trained or have the capability to do much more than follow the herd. Sheep don't set foot out of their comfort zone, do they?

To be successful, you need the mindset of determination focused clearly in your head. People will try and hold you back, whether they mean to or not, but you must prepare for your journey in this world and not walk into a disaster zone where, like sheep, you surround yourself with stress and drudgery, like most people do in life. Time and time again, people who are good at their jobs are promoted and elevated into other jobs that they weren't designed for or adequately trained and supported to do. Because they are technically proficient doesn't mean to say they can do a senior role in the same arena, or a management role, and certainly not without the correct mindset and training being applied.

All too often, good technical people are elevated to management positions that they aren't ready for, and then stress prevails in terms of achieving targets and showing excellent proficiency in the role. Therefore, so many people fail. They also step out of their comfort zone, and they are ill equipped to deal with that kind of leap yet. Their zone of influence also can hold them back with negativity towards a promotion, for example, which inevitably derives from jealousy. Jealousy in your zone of influence is to be expected. In a strange way, you would think that zone of influence would assist you in many ways, but if they see you venturing off down a lane that they don't think is appropriate, then they all get together and have a chat with the intent of getting you back on track. We can't have someone going off in their own direction to do something that we have never done; it's just not allowed. As sheep, we must all stick together, right?

So, the committee will get together and plot a way of getting you back in line and to conform with the hidden, secret, and never spoken about rules of the group. Just try and tell someone in your zone of influence that you don't want to go out this weekend as a group as you normally would, and that you would like to have a relaxing day out with a friend instead, as a change. Panic alarms will go off within the group. Calls will be made to other members of the group, and then at some stage you will receive a call from one of them or a visit to find out what's wrong.

I suppose the secret is to say yes to everything and then to state that you have a lot to do that weekend but will be there if you possibly can. There will still be a committee meeting anyway, but it shows that you are still a part of the zone. I will talk later about creating a new zone of influence, one that is ideal for you, and one that will support you moving forward in your quest, and not one that will hold you back. Friends and colleagues need to support you in your life and working arena, don't they? But do they? Maybe it's time to review friends and work colleagues soon, to determine which ones hold you back and which ones propel you forward.

My Habits Are Not Helping

It's important to understand yourself, and that includes the good and the bad. The good is easy to accept, and the bad is to learn from and improve. Where you are now in your life and business is down to the choices you have made, which have provided the vehicle for you to get where you are in life. But there is more to achieve, and maybe you need to change things around, or maybe this is the start for you. Either way, it's time to look at changing things in your life and, unfortunately, that is going to cause you some discomfort and maybe some pain. But if you start today, then what you start to change now will never be easier than it is today.

If you leave it, then it's simply going to take longer, you will have lost valuable time, and the discomfort will be greater. The reason that the discomfort will be greater is because your old habits will be more deeply embedded within you. It's a bit like a person who suddenly stops exercising and then decides, after 12 months, to run a marathon; that is going to hurt more than ever before, and a lot more than if you simply had never stopped exercising and had kept up with keeping fit and healthy in a positive new way. You have developed plenty of habits that have served you well, but sometimes you must upgrade yourself, like a computer's software, and keep yourself fresh, updated, and moving forward in the way that serves you best.

Goals are destinations, but you need a vehicle to get you there, and new habits can be that vehicle. You need to become the person today that you need to be tomorrow when you wake up. You need to write the script for the person you need to be now, and that means fleshing out the character, from the clothes you wear, to the friends you keep, to the new skills you need to learn, to the mindset you need to adopt and instil in your subconscious. Your new habits will create the framework of the character you are destined to become, and you need to flesh that person out now. If you are in business, this includes what changes are required to move your business forward, and looking after your clients in new ways.

The world is changing every day, and we have the entire planet at our fingertips, so there is no need to think small anymore. Your emails, Facebook comments, Instagram posts, etc. can be seen all around the globe, and you only have to simply connect to make a new impact. It's time to cast aside the old you and think passionately about how you would like the new you to be in this exciting, changing Covid world we are in right now. You are unique, and the globe welcomes uniqueness in every form. There are so many choices in the world that people are craving a new, unique breath of fresh air, and that can be you right now. You can invent yourself once again, but this time it can be truly YOU, based on what is truly inside you and not what has been supplanted by your old zone of influence group or by your old thoughts.

You need to be careful about what you think about, because what you focus on will truly turn up in some form in your life. You have no room for negativity in a world full of abundance. "Ask and you shall receive." Start with this thought as a new habit when you focus on your next move in life. Every cell in your body has intelligence inside, and they are eavesdropping on your every thought. You have no room for a depressing thought; you become what you think about, so my tip to you today is to THINK WISELY.

I Have No Skill Set

By the time we make it into our twenties and thirties, we are possibly saddled with responsibilities and even some financial hardship, which may include debt of some kind (e.g., university loan or simply a mortgage). We may be married and have a family too. Although this sounds too depressing to write, your dreams may have taken a big battering in the first few decades of your life, and sometimes any paying job is acceptable when there are bills to be paid. If a family is already under way, then even more responsibility and financial strain has entered your arena. Sometimes survival itself is an accomplishment, and it's only when you start to get older, and your income starts to improve, that you get an opportunity to take a breath and wonder what hit you over the last few years.

But we simply were not given the skill set whilst at school or in preparation to leave school, to have the ability to think about how we really thought our life could be or should be. Instead, it was THIS IS HOW IT IS and you should simply accept it. Skill set is really another way of saying a human toolkit. Just as a DIY expert may have a garden shed full of tools for every given DIY task that may be asked of them, your skill set is the human version of the DIY toolkit. None of us become a carpenter or electrician overnight, or are able to use tools like a chisel, etc. just like that; instead, there must be a period of information gathering and then plenty of practice sessions to get it right–and guess what–to learn new skills and habits.

For roughly the first twenty years of your life, you were gifted someone else's toolbox, but now you have an opportunity to develop your very own. What goes into your toolbox is dependent upon what you wish to achieve in life, and the new skills/habits you are prepared to learn. If you feel you are lacking in life skills, then similar to when you pass your driving test, the learning adventure all starts now. You must start to use your imagination again. Knowledge can take you from A to B, but remember that imagination can take you everywhere. If you can think it, it can happen.

Everything that you have, came from the invisible world first. You had to think about it before you could manifest it. Your skill set and toolbox need your attention, and it's important to focus on what your passions are in life and to make sure you pursue them. Your life should not be all one way, resulting in you compromising your passions and dreams. It's an opportunity to explore and develop passions/dreams further, and you can do that by taking action and experiencing things first hand. Your skill set toolbox is opened here, right now.

I Have No Support

Sometimes, when they come to see me and discuss their lives or businesses, my clients complain that they have little or no support from friends, family, or colleagues. I sometimes say that no support is better than the wrong support, and there's plenty of poor or negative support and suggestions dished out by over-enthusiastic well-wishers. The key here is to build the right support team for YOU. As one author of a mindfulness book said to me, "You need good scaffolding, David," and he was right. You need a good support team and coaching for your life and in business or your career.

There's no point in talking to your window cleaner about pensions if you want sound advice, unless he's a pension expert too, of course, lol. I once told a prospective client what my fees were, and he said, "I can't afford you," and I told him, "You can't afford not to have me in your world." I said to him, "If within your free initial 30-minute consultation with me, if I can't help you with ideas that will have a financial impact in your life immediately, I will give you 6 one-hour coaching sessions for free."

You need THE RIGHT COACH if you are serious about your life. Even the top coaches have coaches, because at the very least, you need to be held accountable for your actions, and you NEED TO TAKE ACTION. For that reason alone, a coach will be invaluable. Many people think they can read books and coach themselves, but you need a team of support, and it makes the journey more enjoyable as well as successful. And that's the sort of life you want, right? Enjoyable and to be successful? So why ever doubt a proven formula to success? You need to start somewhere, so why not start off with the number one member of your support team: DAVID CHARNOCK. Or, if I'm not available, then I will sort you out in some other way and get you fixed up with one of my proven coaching programs, where my team will coach you to success using my numerous approaches to achieving meteoric success in life and the corporate world. Your journey doesn't end with this book; it's only just the beginning, and you are in line to step up to greatness. Imagine yourself with an unstoppable support team around you … how could you possibly fail? You can't, and you won't, if you are committed to being the best person you can possibly be, and are open to change. It may be painful change initially, but in a short space of time, you will forget your old life and blossom into your new world. Life is for the committed and the brave. If you are neither, then commit to becoming so, because this is not the time to back down from your destiny.

My Toolbox Is Empty

In addition to a good support team, you need to develop your toolbox of available skills and knowledge, and ultimately establish your own economy in life. The days are gone where you can leave school or university and go into a job or career and stay in it till retirement. It is most likely that you will have three or four different careers in your lifetime. If you are ill prepared for change and are reliant upon others for your income, then you are vulnerable, and your life is out of your control. Being dependent upon others as you may be, you are most likely working on their dreams instead of focusing on your own.

Unless you take control of your own life and destiny, someone else will take control of it for you. The first thing you must therefore consider is to develop an additional income, known as a side hustle to your main job. Most people have responsibilities and have little choice other than to keep working hard in their current job, and are locked in by the salary the role provides. An additional income needs to be considered, and this could involve an area that is a pastime or hobby of yours that has a money-making opportunity. This of course takes additional time, valuable time, but if you want to make inroads and give yourself additional life skills and opportunities, then you need to make the effort and find time. If that means getting up an hour earlier to work on your side hustle, then that's what you need to do to make changes in your life.

Getting an education on life has to be a priority, as the first twenty years of your life has probably not served you too well, apart from now being able to operate a calculator. My apologies if you feel I am being overly critical of the state education system, but let me be clear; I am VERY CRITICAL of the state education system. In terms of LIFE SKILLS, please feel free to list some that you feel you now have that are particularly vital and useful for modern day life. You will be able to list a few, but when you get past the basics, you find that you are totally inept and are NONE THE WISER to living and getting ahead in this world.

Money, finance, investing, and pensions is a huge area, and if you have come out of school with a comprehensive knowledge of these topics and not had to pay for this education, then I want to know which school you attended. Let's put it another way: If you had to start school again, what education would you choose for yourself? Think for two minutes and then write down what you feel you would have benefited from learning and knowing, before you left school. Money in this world doesn't guarantee happiness, but it allows you to have options in your life. Money doesn't make you happy, but it can provide you with the power to make choices in your life that could make you ultimately happy, fulfilled, and contented. So, making sure you have enough money in your life is vital.

There may be other things that you have already decided are vital to have in your life too, so what are they? So, if your toolbox is empty, then it's time to start to make a list of essential tools that need to be acquired, and topics that you need to learn, which will improve your education for making the most of this global life you have at your fingertips.

There Is Me Though, Don't Forget

Make no mistake, you have a global empire at your fingertips. The key is to have a key, and be able to unlock the door to the opportunity that you have available. Some people don't see the opportunity. Some people see the opportunity but don't do anything with it. Some people see the opportunity and do the wrong things with it. You need to learn about GOING GLOBAL in a GLOBAL WORLD.

There was a time when I was a teenager and I lived in a small village. With no mobile phones invented yet, it was a painstaking communication issue trying to keep in contact with your friends. Keeping in contact with your friends meant physical activity–either turning up to some shared event or going round to where people lived. Landline telephones were expensive to use back then, and most calls were kept to a minimum timewise. My breakthrough back then was to learn about and harness the use of CB radio. It was basically free, and you had 40 channels that you could use to chat to people in your local area. It was my first taste of freedom and of free communication at the time.

Now all you need is a mobile phone and a line of credit, and you can communicate with the WORLD from the palm of your hand, anytime day or night. You have the world at your feet; however, so do millions of other people around the world. The internet and social media are swamped with people, adverts, and messages. The key is to stand out from the millions, and here is the challenge. You need to stand out, be noticed, be listened to, and be remembered. Suddenly, your education, knowledge, and mindset need to be tuned in and be fit for purpose.

Most people don't have the tools to make the most of the global opportunities that are available in this world, and therefore settle for a life of fear, living out other people's dreams and being controlled as well as manipulated. I run plenty of courses that will lift your education to the level required for success in this world. It is important to keep educating yourself and improving as the world develops. Opportunities exist all around the world, with different economies, countries, and cultures possibly needing your skill set and what you have to offer. Thinking small is a thing of the past now, if you want to make it big.

Global education is required now, and there is so much to learn and so many opportunities available. You need to look beyond your high street for jobs and opportunities, and look with a new focus. When you tune into the news channel now, it's not just about local news; it's about the country's news, and it is kept up to date by the minute. And even world news is being kept up to date for you by the second. The world is a smaller place now than it ever has been, so you need the tools to embrace it successfully.

Learn in the next chapter that it's okay to make mistakes and act like a winner. Learn that choosing your friends wisely is essential and that you only get good answers back to good questions. Find out why surrounding yourself with the right people is essential to your success, and that goals are good, but goals that truly inspire are greater. Also, learn what it truly takes in life to be who you need to be and achieve your dreams.

Questions:

- How often do you follow the crowd and do what everyone else does, despite knowing that you would be happier doing something else? Write down a few examples and then explore why you do this. Does it serve you well? Is it time to change? Is it time to change your friends?

- Are you focused? Do you make sure that you are not easily distracted? Are you careful about what you think? If you attract and manifest things that you think about, isn't it best to think wisely? If you tell yourself you are clumsy, then guess what? You will be ... clumsy. Amazing, isn't it? Write down your thought patterns about yourself, and highlight those that don't serve you well now.

- What new skills, habits, or knowledge do you need to acquire, to pop in and have ready in your new human toolbox (your skill sets)? Remember, things are not hard to learn; they are simply different and maybe you aren't used to them. So, what are your needs? What tools do you need to get you where you truly need to be in your dreams?

- Education is a lifelong habit that you need to embrace and absorb into your mental thought processes. Is it time to consider having your very own personal coach, to be a part of your vital support team and keep you accountable and on track? Call me for a free, non-obligatory chat, and see if the time is right for you to step up and reach your dreams.

Bonus Real Magic Formula:

Real magic rests beyond your current comfort zone. Your comfort zone has been established by your current zone of influence, your family, your friends, your successes/failures, and your education. Your comfort zone needs to change, and you must step out beyond your existing barriers and enter the area of abundance and opportunity. You need to establish a new comfort zone, and your new world sits here awaiting your arrival. Go stretch yourself and see what you can achieve if you take action and have faith.

YOUR NEW COMFORT ZONE IS REAL MAGIC.

Chapter 5

Down But Not Out

5

Making Choices, Making Them Blind

When you have a dubious zone of influence, a sparse toolbox, and have had a limited education, it can feel that you are making decisions and choices blindly in your life. So, what can you do when you are starting out, when you are repairing your life and improving the areas that will take you forward in life? Well, part of the problem can be that you don't know you have a dubious zone of influence, a sparse toolbox, and a limited education. It starts when you feel that something isn't quite right in your life, that something doesn't quite fit, and that some days are just slipping by with little or no significance. Your life is lacking substance, and perhaps inspiration, or a spark that fires up your belly and gets you excited at the start of each new day.

This isn't a sign that your life is a disaster or that it's time to throw yourself face down in the river; it's more like a sign for you to take stock of your life and take a moment—a genuine, long moment, and an opportunity to go inwards to consider your truest, deepest feelings—to ask yourself, the operator, the person behind the eyes, the observer to your life that always follows you around and offers guidance occasionally, to pause and reconnect with the power source that is REALLY YOU. You were born connected to this source; you came and arrived from this ultimate source, and now it's time to plug back in and continue your journey, your destiny, and your reason for being here.

Now how exciting is this? You have this ability, and the way to access this tool, this facility, is to find a quiet spot, sit, relax, gently close your eyes, and focus on your breath. Sink into yourself and enter the silence between the breaths, and engage with your source. The source, the universe, a spiritual connection, religion—whatever you want to call it, and whatever it feels to you, THEN THAT'S WHAT IT IS. This will be your new habit, and it will become your library; when you need direction, guidance, or a sign, maybe a nudge or reassurance, it will be there for you.

It has always been there for you. It was a gift given to you from the universe, and it has been with you on your journey ALWAYS. It will be a habit that you will need to develop, and you will eventually treasure the day you reconnected to your true self—the self that is magical, mysterious, and that lives on in the spiritual world when your material self has long expired on this Earth. You are a spiritual being, having a human experience. It could even be said that you are on vacation and your purpose is to simply EXPERIENCE. EXPERIENCE EVERYTHING by ACTION.

Taking action and experiencing is a magical gift, and it's there to be used and used and used. You will make mistakes, of course; who said you shouldn't, couldn't, or wouldn't? Do you learn more through making mistakes, or by getting everything right? When you get things right, I think you praise yourself and dwell in gratitude for yourself at how well you have done or how clever you are. But when you make mistakes, so much more happens; magic happens. That magic is education, that gut rot feeling you experience when things go wrong and force you to think in the NOW, and to wake up from the dream you live each day, to stop, reflect, and learn from the process.

Unfortunately, we overstep the mark; instead of just learning from the cock-up, we decide to beat ourselves up about the mistakes we have made. It's as if our expectation is that we should get everything right 100%, despite not having any point of reference or guidebook.

We need to be kind to ourselves, to be grateful and to celebrate our experience, both good and not so good. TRUST ME.

Following the Crowd

I have always been a big boxing fan. I always have been since my father introduced me to boxing, with tales of listening to big fights on the radio, beaming in from America to the UK, in the earlier hours of the morning when he was a child. In 2003, I was on tour in America. I had decided to take some time off and had chosen to fly to the states and tour 5 major cities. One of those destinations was Las Vegas. I had always wanted to visit Las Vegas—"Viva Las Vegas."

What do you think about when you think about Las Vegas? I always think about gambling, Bugsy Siegel, Elvis, the Rat Pack, and world championship boxing ... oh, and a lady called Margaret Randall. Margaret who? Margaret told me to go to Vegas; she said the place was amazing and that I would love it, and that two weeks would never be enough, and to go for a month. So I did (thank you, Margaret). She is a great, amazing lady, who impacted my life more than she knows, and she has a great husband and family too.

It was November 2003, and even if you don't like or agree with boxing, you need to listen to this story. I had always wanted to attend a world title boxing fight in Vegas, but to be honest, I never thought it would happen. Resting on my bed, in a hotel on Las Vegas Boulevard, I grabbed a *What's On* magazine and thumbed through what was on that week. Suddenly, the page exploded in my face when I read that Antonio "The Magic Man" Tarver was fighting the ruthless Roy Jones Junior, at the Mandalay Bay Casino on Saturday night.

I grabbed the hotel phone and rang the hotline for tickets. To my amazement, there were still some left, and although they were not great tickets, I bought one and I was IN. I was IN. The fight was called

"NOW IT'S PERSONAL," and for me ... NOW IT WAS. It was meant to be, and I was going. I was so excited, I simply couldn't contain myself, and I messaged my father immediately and told him I was going to a fight in Vegas. He was so excited too, and it was like I had his presence with me, enjoying the moment too.

I'm not sure why, but I decided to go down to check out the Mandalay Bay Casino the night before the fight. It was about 9 p.m. on Friday, November 7th, 2003, and I arrived at the casino with my backpack on and my movie camera. I had decided to take my movie camera with me at all times, because you never knew when something worth recording would pop up in your face; and historically, I had always missed out on recording significant moments in my life. The casino and hotel was amazing, and not only was there a boxing fight taking place that weekend, but I believe a rodeo championship was also happening, which would explain the hundreds of people wearing cowboy hats everywhere.

As I walked around the casino complex, I took it all in, and there were promotional banners up everywhere for the big fight the next night. I was always a person for investigating places and wondering what is around the corner, so I had to explore. I suddenly stumbled across a rear reception area in the Mandalay Bay Hotel and Casino, and to my amazement, they had erected a mini boxing ring to promote the big Tarver/Jones clash. So, I sat down and took out my movie camera to do a little recording and to take it all in.

It's to Be Expected

I grabbed a local newspaper and decided to sit for a while and take in the atmosphere. The back page of the newspaper was all about the Tarver/Jones fight. Suddenly, two guys walked into the hotel and went to the reception desk to check in. I studied them intently, and although they had their backs to me, I could have sworn one of them was

Antonio "The Magic Man" Tarver. If it were him, then this too would be magic. So, I also went over to the desk, and I placed my newspaper on the counter, looking at the back page all about the fight. The tall 6'2 guy turned to me and said, "Who do you think will win the fight?" "My money is on the last man standing," I said. He smiled and laughed, and then I held my hand out to him and he took it.

I was shaking the hand of the "Magic Man" himself, Antonio Tarver. Trying not to be stage struck, I attempted to talk with him about his chances in the fight. He had all the time in the world for me, and claimed that he would stop Jones late in the fight. As we chatted, I suddenly remembered I had my movie camera in my backpack, so I asked Antonio if we could do an Ali rant together. He looked puzzled and said, "You want me to do what dude?" "An Ali rant," I said. He still looked confused, until I told him that Mohammad Ali would always record a rant before each of his fights, claiming victory before he had ever stepped in the ring. With my movie camera in my hand, I turned the viewfinder to face both myself and the Magic Man, and he started his victory rant. The guy was amazing, and I have that footage today and will eventually show it on my website for all to see.

The day of the fight arrived, and it will come as no surprise to you to know that I was back at the casino in more than plenty of time; and again, I was snooping all over the place. The casino was packed, and the press and security were everywhere. I found myself in the basement areas of the Mandalay complex, and suddenly I walked through a door into a room full of people, chairs, and a large promotional backdrop. I had just accidently walked into a fight press conference. Without the correct credentials, I was politely asked to leave. I did so, and I headed for the escalator to return to the casino floor. But then, just then, another magic moment happened.

I glanced over at the escalator that was going down to the basement, and on it was a guy who had created a world event in Africa, on October 30th, 1974. I would have been 8 that year. He had been one of the stars of "The Rumble in the Jungle," an event that had been televised to a reported 1 billion viewers around the world. The Rumble in the Jungle was a historic boxing event held in Zaire, between the heavyweight champion of the world, George Foreman, and the challenger, Muhammad Ali, the former heavyweight champion of the world.

As he stepped off the escalator, I was soon shaking hands with the hardest hitting man on the planet, GEORGE FOREMAN. He was so polite and a man who had the softest hands I had ever touched. AMAZING. George lost that fight to Ali in the Congo, and it was one of the biggest upsets in boxing since I could remember. Unfortunately, later that day in Vegas, Tarver lost too, with a dubious points decision to Roy Jones Junior. The crowd booed at the end, thinking Tarver had done enough to get the decision.

You Have Unrealistic Expectations

Muhammad Ali had done more than enough to win the fight with Foreman; he had knocked him out. It had been one of the greatest comebacks in boxing history. Ali had regained the heavyweight champion of the world crown again, against all odds. Whether you like, agree, or disagree with boxing, I suggest you watch the movie, *When We Were Kings*. It is the story of the greatest comeback, and the greatest fight against the odds there had ever been in boxing. Ali had regained his crown as champion, but how had he done it? This is a story about destiny, mindset, goals, habits, role playing, confidence, and total belief. Even Ali's fans and close friends questioned the former champ's ability to win the fight.

George Foreman had destroyed every boxer he had entered the ring with, and normally within 3 rounds. The hardest hitting boxer on the planet, Foreman, was 4/1 on favourite to destroy Ali, but the former champion told his trainer, Angelo Dundee, that he had a secret plan to beat Foreman. Clearly, Ali was motivated to take this challenge, and it had nothing to do with money. His role in life was simple: He wanted to be THE GREATEST. "The greatest" must face challenges and step up to the plate. He had to find a way to win, and there's always a way to win. You must act and be like a winner, never doubting yourself and your ability. He had written the script, and he had to get into character to play the role of the winning fighter. Is it as simple as that? Probably not, but his tactics and his training regime matched the script and his role.

It was difficult to see how anything went wrong at all for Ali in this fight. We have a lot to learn from sports people: dedication beyond what you can imagine, and tactics mixed with a good script and a role to act out. We tend not to see the days, weeks, months, and years of training and dedication. Instead, we see the one-off performance and wonder how this amazing feat was achieved by this person. When you are at one with yourself and in the zone, great things can happen with ease. Great habits achieve GREAT GOALS. Once your habits are developed and in place, you can start to move forward with the new you, which has the capability of achieving the goals you desire.

Motivation will never be in question when you have established the goals that are right for you, goals that get you inspired and excited. If you aren't excited to get up in the morning to work on your goals, then they aren't the goals for you. Dump them and get new ones. It's that simple. If you try to achieve goals that don't get you excited, then you won't achieve them, and you are simply wasting your vital time and your life. You can't afford to waste your time, so don't do it at all costs. Learn from sports people; google a few, and add them to your zone of influence. Study them and get to know everything about them and what motivates them. Try to understand what their goals are and what habits they keep. Study them so closely, like you were going to play them in a film, and see how dedicated they are to success and doing what's necessary to win.

Athletic stars don't just wake up and become Olympic medal holders. In business, you need to study successful people and see how they made it big. There is no need to reinvent the wheel again. See how millionaires operate and become mega successful. What are their traits, their habits, their goals, their loves and their passions? It's all there for the careful, observing eye to catch and record.

We Would All Love to Be Happy

There are several difficulties we must face on the journey to greatness or success or contentment, and that is the feeling of being undermined or sucked back into your comfort zone by your zone of influence. Countless times when I would discuss my ideas or plans with the wrong person, I would get the response, "We would all love to travel the world, but we have to work for a living," or "Do you not think we would have done that if we could?" Or just a general response, "We would all love to be happy!!" When you talk to the wrong person about your plans, it ends up being a tiring, undermining experience that leaves you deflated and questioning your own plans and ability.

Your plans get challenged by all jealous and non-achieving individuals, and then you end up spending most of your time trying to justify your dreams and ambitions. As soon as that happens, the feelings of self-doubt creep in, and you start to question yourself and start agreeing with the people who have probably never done anything with their lives. Therefore, children can sometimes end up being like their parents. As some parents unfortunately fail to achieve in life, they pass this "nonachievement skill" down to their offspring. And when people begin to realise that they have developed this nonachievement skill, to justify doing nothing in their life, they decide to invent A REASON WHY THEY COULDN'T ACHIEVE.

You very rarely hear someone taking responsibility for their own actions and truthfully declaring why they failed to do something with their life. So, if your zone of influence is packed to the rafters with nonachievers, then you better watch out and take action on a massive scale to blast through this apathetic wall of discouragement and despondency. On the other hand, when you get a person listening to your dreams, who is on the same wavelength, then it's like a breath of fresh air. It doesn't have to be a successful person either; just someone who genuinely cares about you and wants the best for you.

Encouragement to expand on your ideas, goals, and dreams, can be an immensely powerful session. If the truth be known, it's what you would ask me to do for you. Most of my clients are starting from scratch in personal or corporate development situations, and have done extraordinarily little inward analysis of themselves, nor given themselves a chance to think openly and honestly about life in general. There's no better person to have in your team than me, as your life or business coach. You need to be asked the right questions so that you give yourself the RIGHT ANSWERS.

Remember when I mentioned about my careers advisor offering me a career in the Army, and THAT'S IT?!! When teenagers are asked about their career and what they want to be, they can come out with obvious answers, such as a professional footballer, a dentist, an artist, etc., but the question must be somewhat different. Assuming you have a suitable skill for football, then maybe the question should be, "What are you prepared to do to become a professional footballer?" Then suddenly you start to give yourself answers and information on what YOU NOW NEED TO DO.

It's Three Steps Forward and Four Back

When your coach asks you the right questions, your life starts to take shape, and your future looks more exciting, realistic, achievable, and inspirational. Clarity is vital; the clearer the goal, the easier you can make your new goal setting habits. All too often, people don't think they need a coach; they feel they can sort things out alone and are confident that they can take themselves from A to B. The truth is that for most people, THEY WILL FAIL. You need to firstly understand where "A" is. To be able to leave "A," you must first know where you are, to know that you have left!! Then you need to understand what it's going to take to get you *to* "B." '"To" is the journey, the route, the direction, your life. Sometimes it's not all about "B"; it's about the journey—because getting to "B" may take you 20 years, so "to" has to be an amazing journey, doesn't it? Also, "B" may change along the journey because discoveries along the way may change your passions, and therefore your goal may need to be flexible.

You need help, and even if you used a coach just to make you accountable, it would be the best investment you have ever made. While you are trying to enjoy your life or enjoy running your business, trying to change things can simply be too much for you. There's simply too much to do. Your life and your business need an assistant, and if you are committed to moving forward, you need to make this investment. Trust me, YOU CAN'T AFFORD NOT TO. Without the support of an assistant or coach, you may make some progress in certain areas; but without an organised, accountable, committed approach, you may well fail in other vital areas that are needed to make the difference for you to achieve your goals.

It may well feel like 3 steps forward and four steps back—minimal successes and maximum frustrations with setbacks. Why? Because we are human, and our lives are so busy, simply trying to stand still and keep up with the pace of life. We mean well, and we want to succeed; truly we do, but it's no better sometimes than choosing New Year's resolutions. A few weeks down the road, you will have probably even forgotten what they were, never mind achieved them. Anyone who scorns the very thought of New Year's resolutions, is probably like that because they have never achieved anything positive from having them. Diets are always top of the agenda straight after Christmas, and discounted gym memberships are always marketed to the max at this time. January starts off busy for gyms, but come February, they are considerably quieter because people simply don't follow through on their goals. They pay big membership fees, and even money can't keep them focused and on their path to a healthier body and mind. You need a team around you, and you need to invest in it now.

In the next chapter, you will learn the importance of becoming authentic, and finding the true self that resides inside of us all but sometimes is seen very seldom. Now is the time to find the real you, and to find out how to harness success.

Questions:

- It's okay to make mistakes, right? No? But how do you learn? List out on a page all the things that have gone, shall we say, not to plan, and then list out what you have learned from that process. You will find that your greatest mistakes are your greatest teachers. Mistakes are a part of life and are one of our best educational tools.

- Look at some of your goals that you have set for yourself in the past and have not achieved. Why is that? Were there good reasons, or were you simply setting goals that failed to inspire you? Write a page of targets you have failed to follow up on, and discuss with yourself why this has happened.

- Let's consider your zone of influence circle, meaning your friends, colleagues, and general social spectrum. This is a critical exercise, so you need to be honest with yourself. Take a piece of paper and write a list of your zone of circle contacts, and then I want you to write on the right side, next to each name, what they contribute to your life. Are they a support, a positive influence, a negative influence, or an energy zapper? Then decide who is important to you and who should be dispensed with immediately. Also look at any gaps you may have, and put a plan in place to add to your support team.

• When we look at blockages in our lives, to moving forward and achieving our goals, quite often we don't ask ourselves the right questions. We need to get focused and to simply get to the bottom of why we don't follow through on our tasks; are we choosing the wrong goals for ourselves? So, I want you to ask yourself these two questions: A. What will it take for you to achieve your top goal? And then, B. What will be the consequences or feeling if you don't achieve this goal? Ponder your answers for a moment.

Bonus Real Magic Formula:

Be thankful for the challenges that show up in your life, because you learn more in those moments. We all make mistakes, but we all view making mistakes differently. Mistakes wake you up and educate you. Don't be frightened or hesitant to try new things. Say yes to more, and learn from the good things you achieve, but especially learn from the bad choices or mistakes. When you take action and experience the effects, you are truly alive.

TAKING MASSIVE ACTION AND
LEARNING FROM THE PROCESS IS REAL MAGIC.

Chapter 6

None the Wiser

6

It's Not My Fault

We have discussed a lot of critical areas of our lives in the first five chapters of this book, but be under no illusion; it is not intended to reflect badly on you, or to criticise you in any way for the life you have currently, or for any of your current issues. All we can do is our best at the time. None of us were born with a magic wand or an idiot's guidebook for our lives. So, we do our best. But now that you realise the basic problems in life, it's time to decide what you wish to do about it, and to decide what's next for you in this life. And before you start looking back over your life with rose-coloured spectacles, or being overly critical of some of your earlier decisions, YOU MUST STOP RIGHT NOW.

This is the first day of the remainder of your life. Whether you are 15 years old or 50, each day of your life is precious, and it's important to live it the way you were meant to, being you and authentic. We need to spend time and focus on those areas that we can affect and change to suit our new role in life, or if we aren't sure yet on a role, we need to make critical steps in our exciting new direction. It's time to cut ourselves a great deal of slack, and to stop finding fault with some of our previous decisions and actions in life. We are here together, on this journey together, and we will accomplish a new life for ourselves, where faults and failures are simply learning opportunities and educational memos to ourselves.

When we stop crucifying ourselves for our actions and decisions, we start to learn. Imagine if I told you now that you weren't allowed to make another mistake for the rest of your life. Now, that would be a task, a burden, an uncomfortable rule, which you would start to hate and fear. So now I'm telling you that you are allowed to try things, have new experiences, see how they feel, see if you are good at them, and enjoy them; see if you are passionate about them and can excel at them in life. And when you try these new experiences, it's okay to totally mess up. Messing up is something to learn from, and you can enjoy the learning process. Learning opportunities are opportunities to improve, and to take the highs with the lows.

You can only appreciate a real high in your life when you have been dealt a real low. You then appreciate the journey; the sun is amazing and hot, but only when you have experienced the cold and the wet. The magic will arrive when you are ready to receive it and appreciate it, but it won't materialise until you are completely ready to receive it. "When the pupil is ready, the teacher will arrive." If you believe, you will receive; you will attract what you think about, so it's so important to think carefully and stick to the agenda you have set for your life.

But what is my agenda, I hear you say? What on Earth does life have in store for me; what's next? A neighbour of mine went to work thinking the same thing last week when he agreed to help his builder friend replace a flat roof on a home in the village. The sun was shining, and all was right with the world; however, someone had decided that this was going to be his last day on this Earth. His age was only just above a half century when he went into cardiac arrest and never regained consciousness again.

I Didn't Join the Wrong Queue

I watched a YouTube video some years ago, when the actor Mike Myers, star of Austin Powers, met his idol, Deepak Chopra. I think they hit the stage together, talking about life in general, but it was what Deepak said that has stayed with me till this day. When talking about life and death, Deepak said that the grim reaper always walks with you and remains only three paces behind you at all times. We all die, but there are two things that are unknown: (1) the date of your demise/death, and (2) the method of execution. It sounds morbid and it sounds obvious, but all too often, people just don't get the inevitability of (1) and (2).

People live their lives as if they have joined a different queue/line to everyone else. They act as if this life is going to go on for decades, and that they are immune from stress, illness, and ultimately death. But surely, we all accept that WE WILL DIE? Yes, of course, WE WILL ALL DIE, BUT IT WILL NEVER BE TOMORROW. If not you, we all know people who think like this and take life for granted. We don't mean to; we simply don't want to accept that we will die—it always happens to someone else, doesn't it? Most of us are living in a dream each day. We join the queue/line of life and, without much thought, make it our very own, and we follow some others person's path. I'm going to draw your attention to a song by Jackson Browne, called "For a Dancer." Feel free to research the lyrics of the song, but for our purpose, I will pick out the following verses that stand out to me, and I hope they do to you also.

Just do the steps that you've been shown
By everyone you've ever known
Until the dance becomes your very own
No matter how close to yours
Another's steps have grown
In the end, there is one dance you'll do alone

Into a dancer you have grown
From a seed somebody else has thrown
Go on ahead and throw some seeds of your own
And somewhere between the time you arrive
and the time you go
May lie a reason you were alive, but you'll never know

It's time to stop joining other people's lines/queues, and instead of following, it's time to start leading. It's time to hit the front in the race of life, and reach out, stretch out, be a front runner in life, and take this race by the scruff of the neck, dictating the direction that's right for you. Let people follow you for a change. You will need support along the way, and these people can help you while they help themselves to their own direction.

Thank Goodness I Woke up!

The great news is that you HAVE WOKEN UP. You have awakened from your slumber, so give thanks to yourself that this has happened while so many remain blinkered and blind. You will walk tall, and you will walk FREE. Now imagine you were going to write a guidebook for mankind to read, digest, and implement on how to live a life full of REAL MAGIC and to MANIFEST your BEST 24/7. Where would it start, and what ingredients are needed now to bake this cake we are looking at baking, which will set us free and give us the life we have always wanted? In a book, you need an introduction and chapters that take you to the conclusion required, while a cake requires ingredients and a strategy if it is to be a success and taste amazing.

When you look at amazing athletes, they haven't got to this level by accident. It took planning, mindset, strategy, diet, and application. Just like when you baked this cake or made a meal, there were the ingredients, cooking instructions, what gets mixed with what, how long it gets cooked for, and at what temperature. So, in general, to be a success, you need to have: CLEAR FOCUS – EDUCATION – INGREDIENTS – STRATEGY – OUTCOME – REVIEW.

Clear focus determines what you want and why you want it. We will go into detail later. *Education* is about researching your topic, and what you want to do in life. *Ingredients* is like baking a cake, but in life it's all about what component parts you use to make this a wonderful success. *Strategy* is about how you need to go about baking the cake, assembling, and using the ingredients. Some things need to be done in the correct order for success to materialise. *Outcome* is getting the results you wanted and need. Are they the outcomes you expected? The *Review* lets you check the entire process and determine what needs to change to improve the outcome. Was the cake too sweet, did it have too much sugar in it, or was it over cooked?

You will have the ability to tweak all those areas that go together to make the magic happen. Only a small tweak can make the difference and make your life 100% improved. It's quite strange that when a toddler is trying to learn to walk and falls over a few times, the parents don't turn around and say, "Oh, that's it, our child isn't a walker; they can't walk!!" No, instead they persist and support the child until they take their first steps and, ultimately and eventually, start to walk. How crazy would that be if we just gave up? But in life, it happens, and we give up on things and just mentally tell ourselves, "I just can't do it." Think of all the things you were taught to do when you were small, and now imagine if people had given up on you. How would it have been in life for you? Our perception shapes everything, and we must learn to change our perception when it's not in our favour. Remember, *if you change the way you look at things, the things you look at change.*

What Do I Do Next?

When I coach people, some of whom are already phenomenally successful, at our first meeting, we normally discuss exactly "WHY ARE YOU HERE?" Why did you decide to arrange this meeting? What are you committed to getting out of our sessions, for you, your career, and your family? These are big questions, and ones that require you to consider very deeply and thoroughly. There is a powerful force inside every person, and your life's mission is to connect with and unleash this magic into your new world. Sometimes, now is the time to relax and try to connect with this force. It's inside you, but the waters are deep and murky, and we must set off in search of the real you, the invisible life force that is truly you ... and so the quest for magic begins.

To relax and go within successfully, we must first ignore or cut out the everyday clutter and clanging that is your current everyday life. You have so many thoughts, worries, distractions, and roles to play each day, it's no wonder you are confused, lost, and muddled. A relaxing meditation is required at this stage, and it's the only way to get in charge of your brain. It's like an out-of-control elephant let loose in a shopping mall, with people taking cover and watching the drama unfold. You need to find your quiet place, so lock the office door, put up the out-of-office sign, or take refuge in the garden shed. I should say that this is best done in a coaching environment, so feel free to call me ... I will respond.

A deep breathing meditation is required, so if you haven't done this before or are sceptical, then get in touch with me without delay. The purpose of this meditation is to calm your brain down and take back control. You weren't meant to exhaust yourself each day in this way, so now let's stop it. Simply sink into the chair, relax, and become aware of every limb and muscle touching the chair. Take a big breath in and sink further into the chair. Just let go, and I want you to start to use your visual skills and imagination. What skills, I hear you say? Well, you have them, and if you've never used them before, or think you can't, then hang on to your britches.

If you don't think you can visualise, then I want you to tell me the colour of your front door. I also want you to tell me the position of the lock on your front door, and the location of your house number or name on the property. The chances are that if you have answered all these questions, you can visualise, because to answer these questions, you most probably had a vision of your front door in your mind. Did you? Then you can visualise. If you didn't, then relax and try again. It will happen for you after a few tries.

Now I want you to imagine/visualise yourself relaxing in the chair. Start to massage every muscle in your body, starting at the top of your head, soothing out all the tension from the day. The importance here is to relax your tension and to start getting your breath under control. Start to become aware of your breathing. You don't have to think about breathing, because it all gets done for you automatically; but we are going to take charge and tell the body that we need to be the boss for the moment, and get your breathing into a controlled, relaxed state. If you need help on meditation, then get in touch, or google a simple, straightforward one for relaxation purposes.

Where Am I?

Once relaxed, it's about visualising who you are and what you want from life now. When I did this on myself many years ago, the following happened for me. First, I didn't find it easy to relax and had to have several tries before I felt I could switch off and calm my brain. I then started to think about my perfect location; I started to create it in my mind. It was a wonderfully warm day; there were lots of green trees and blossoms out, and I was sitting down by a wonderful, slow-moving river, watching the ducks feed, and smelling all the flowers, grass, and morning dew while listening to the birds twittering. I visualised myself creating and walking into this scene.

It was perfect, but it wasn't a scene. It was real; I was there, all provided at no extra cost by my mind. I could touch the grass, smell the blossoms, hear the birds sing, and relax to the sound of water gently flowing by. It was my perfect spot, and I was there. My spirit, my true self, had created the magic, and I was there whilst my body was back in the office on a lunch break. I sat down on the riverbank and I dreamt further about the person I was and what I loved to do. The sun was so warm that day, and this relaxed me even further. I had no worries; I had nothing to do that day but sit and relax and enjoy the moment.

As I thought things through, it became apparent that I needed to work less in my life. Why was I working and stressing each day when I could look at my finances and work out another way of operating. I also needed to be out of the town and into the countryside. I loved nature, and nature nourished my soul, and I needed nourishment. Like baking a cake, folks, to get what you want, you need the right ingredients, strategy, and apparatus for success. With this relaxing deep meditation, I was unlocking my soul, and locating and then stepping inside to my special magical room; a room in which I had left all my life's guidebooks and tools. They may be a little dusty, but they are here, and they are all mine.

Did you notice the location of this room? How did we get here then? Did it just materialise out of thin air? I am going to teach you to find this room, your special magical room, when you need it. I'm going to show you where it is located for you, and how to unlock the door, but you need to trust me. Do you trust me? Imagine having the treasure map to your soul, where X does mark the spot, and then when you get there, I will give you the key to the door. At the moment, you are NONE THE WISER, but you have started to awaken, and this journey to discover your magic will turn you into YOU, which is always THE WISER.

This is not simply a journey into guided meditation. This is so much more, so keep reading, and the magic will start to reveal itself as we progress into unravelling the guidebook of life, which should have been provided at birth, discussed at schools, and taught so that you can understand yourself. Until you begin to know the true you, any other education is pointless. The magical basic YOU, is the foundation for life, from which your journey and education can start. Bless you, for you have started your journey.

Who Am I?

The great, amazing, unravelling and magical journey that you have embarked upon now, is a true journey of discovery. You are whoever you say you are, and whoever you want to be in life. You are not fixed to the spot; you aren't restricted in any way, and you can stop your journey at any given moment and reinvent yourself. Now, how is that for a sales advert? You can reinvent yourself at any given moment. The truth is that you reinvent yourself each day, every day, but the unfortunate bit is that you are reinventing the same person practically each day. You are choosing to wake up as the same person every morning, doing practically the same things all the time, and you wonder why you feel frustrated and unfulfilled at times.

Change is something that can't stop occurring in life, yet we feel that we are unable to change ourselves. Just get out a family photograph album and take a look at a photo of yourself five years ago. We keep changing, whether we want to or not, or whether we like it or not. It's a gift, if we could only wake up and realise it. Who wants to be the same each day, doing the same things day after day? You are fluid and ever changing, and recreating, so this is your chance to discover the real YOU and step in to being with nature. Being at one with nature will allow you to connect with the universe. Who you are is who you want yourself to be, and as you develop and travel along your path, you will evolve, change, and wish to explore different situations and feelings, which will change you whether you like it — or want it—or not.

Death is change too, and we will all physically die at some stage, which we tend to accept but never believe it will happen tomorrow. Don't fall into the trap of putting yourself in a pigeonhole. People like to do this to each other, and it's only done to help us understand where we are with each other, but it's simply not real. YOU ARE NOT FIXED HERE, and you never, ever, ever, ever will be, so wake up and realise that WHO YOU ARE is fluid and NEVER FIXED. So get ready to start embracing change and becoming who you want to be, which may change on a regular basis or even as regular as you wish it to change. Now how amazing is that to know? Do you believe it? No!!!!!! Keep reading then.

Your magic carpet ride starts in the next chapter when you realise that imagination has no boundaries, and neither do you. It's time to experience and feel life, and by taking action, you learn and ultimately succeed.

Questions:

* It's time to wake up and be yourself and be authentic. Forget horoscopes; what are your natural traits? List out who you think you are at this very moment. Are you happy, optimistic, sad, despondent, or motivated on certain aims and goals? Take it to a good friend and ask them how they see you today, and see if they match up, and in which areas. See if you see yourself as you really are to others, or is that a role you play? Do you need to change your role and invent a new one? Who are you? Childhood dreams

and aspirations are also a good area to think about. Have you stepped off your true path, or simply drifted off into the wilderness? Explore your thoughts with a good friend, and try to find the many roles of YOU.

- We have no idea how long we have on this Earth, and we have no way of knowing how we will die, but we know, one day, this will most certainly happen. List out what you must have accomplished before you die. What is so important for you to do before your energy levels start to dip? Whatever age you are, write out how long you think you have left to live, and then look at what you may look like and what energy you will have left when you reach certain ages. All you know is the NOW. Anything in the future is a gamble, but we plan all the same. Don't gamble your life away; start achieving what you need to, on your to-do-before-I-die list.

- Start meditating. Join a class or buy a book. This will connect you to who you really are, and to the exciting but calming silence that exists inside of you, which is filled with REAL MAGIC. Ask the universal silence, which exists inside you, questions as you meditate. Focus on a question, and repeat like a mantra, before listening to the silence inside you, and wait to feel any response or guidance back to you from within. You will manifest guidance from the invisible. Write down what feelings you experience from this process.

- Find your place. Meditation should be conducted regularly. It's your connection to your source, and your way of calming the day's distractions, and reconnecting with you and the universe. Find your sanctuary, a place where you can be quiet and peaceful before and after a busy day. You need just 10 minutes per session, so give yourself 20 minutes a day to find "you" and reconnect. Keep a log of all your sessions and thoughts. Remember to ask the universe questions, and to record what responses you receive in return.

Bonus Real Magic Formula:

You must wake up and seize the day. Finding "you" and being authentic is essential, so build your life from firm foundations. One essential firm foundation you must establish is to connect with a gift provided by the planet. The planet has an abundance of magic, but the biggest one is that of WATER. Health is wealth, and you need to make sure you stay hydrated; your body's water content is maximised to eradicate toxins and keep you in a peak health state.

PURE WATER PROVIDED BY THE PLANET IS REAL MAGIC.

Chapter 7

Rules of the Game

7

I Wasn't Issued with Any Instructions!!

Although we came into this world with no guidebook, our magical purpose resides in our minds, and our minds reside in every speck of electrical energy, in every molecule of our bodies. Our brains are there to be an Earth guide; however, our minds are who we truly are in this universe, and our magical quest is to unlock the code to reach ourselves once more and to think free and live life. We want to wake up inspired and find more purpose, focus, and energy in life. We want to be successful in our lives and careers, and to be genuinely happy. When I coach people, I want to improve their lives, their businesses, and their well-being. This is my calling, my purpose in life—it's that simple. I need to do it; it runs through every vein in my body, and I couldn't change it even if I wanted to, because it sits in my mind, my DNA, and is God/universally given to me. Why try and go against the universal flow?

Our aim should be to connect with the universal flow and to absorb ourselves in all its richness and offerings. They are free for us all, and were meant for you to have at day 1 of your life; however, we became disconnected from our true purpose in life and the lineage that is truly ours and divine. Never forget that success is a choice!! All you need to do is change your mindset and change your role. You must harness the power of possibility, and start to think big, truly huge, maybe even enormous, gigantic scale thoughts that will blow your brain apart so much, and it will be so exciting that it will make you quiver from top to toe. Until Roger Bannister broke the four-minute

93

mile in athletics, no one had!! One person believed it was possible, and then 10 people chased his tail.

You must relax, imagine, and manifest your dreams, and then believe in the power of possibility. All things are possible, aren't they? We let things get in the way of our dreams, and then they fall to one side, and then dust gathers and gathers until your dreams are out of sight and long forgotten. Don't let dust settle on your dreams, people!! Dreams should continue to change, develop, evolve, and become new improved dreams as you conquer, achieve, and develop. An evolving dream never gathers dust.

"An evolving dream never gathers dust."
– David Ian Charnock

There are secrets to living it large and, in this chapter, we shall cover them all, and juice you up, ready to embark more freely on your divine future enriched with purpose, belief, and pure inspiration. The only problem you will ever have in life is YOU. Remember this and write it down to pin to your fridge:

You are the only problem
you will ever have.

However,

you are also the solution!!

So, do you want to be the problem or the solution? You are free to choose. It's that simple, folks. Tomorrow, we can wake up and together change the world.

"Tomorrow, we can wake up and together change the world."
– David Ian Charnock

Where Can I Get an Operator's Guide for Me?

I'm going to say something crazy now, and I will lose some of you. Don't worry, have faith!! Remember, we all need faith, and now is a good time to consume a large amount of it. I want you to get a magic carpet!! Yes, you heard me right, a magic carpet. When I was a child, my older sister, Karen, would play a game with me. She asked me once, as a child, "Do you want a ride on the magic carpet?" Like the Arabian knights who had magical flying carpets in the films and cartoons, my sister had apparently acquired one, and I was amazed. We went off to the lounge and, sure enough, in front of the fire was our hearthrug, which my sister was now telling me had magical powers.

You must believe she told me as we began to sit cross-legged on this now amazing rug. I took front position on our newly acquired travelling device, and my sister sat behind, wrapping her arms around my waist, ready for apparent take off. She told me, however, that there were operational rules for this carpet to fly, and you must always keep your eyes closed tight. I excitedly agreed, and we both closed our eyes shut and held on tightly, fearing we may fall and hurt ourselves. "Where would you like to go?" Karen asked. I was amazed and said, "I'm happy to go anywhere, but let's travel down our street and over the fields."

We held on, we imagined, and with Karen's detailed description, we started to vertically take off magically through the ceiling and then the roof, until we saw daylight and the clouds. Hanging on together, we travelled at top speed, riding the carpet thermals, swaying left and right, until we were over the rooftops and then off into the countryside. I will never forget my sister's magic carpet. It was amazing; the two of us were magically airborne, free like the birds, and flying high in our imaginations. So, people, you need your very own magic carpet.

> Remember:
> Knowledge will take you
> from A to B,
> but
> imagination will take you EVERYWHERE!!

So, where can I purchase my very own magic carpet? I can provide you with your very own magic carpet if you want one. Lots of people will use yoga mats or household rugs, but I can provide you with a truly magical one, blessed with NONE THE WISER magic dust, which is also Covid-free and won't require you to take a vaccine before travelling. In fact, you won't even need a passport, because true magical travel was never designed to be so restrictive, my friends; it really wasn't. "So why would we want a magic carpet, and what benefit will it give us? I think you have lost your mind, Mr. Charnock, and I'm about to stop reading!!"

I get it; I know how you feel and what you are thinking, but your magic carpet is essential. You see, to truly find yourself and your mind, you need first to LOSE YOUR MIND. I want you to lose your mind right now, and we will do it together. I want you to rent out and watch the movie, *Indiana Jones and the Final Crusade*. They are great movies, aren't they? And the magical connection between Harrison Ford and Sean Connery was brilliantly put together by Steven Spielberg. Feel free to watch the whole movie and be carried away by Steven's imagination, because that's what it is. If you don't have time, and you want to go straight to my favourite scene, then fast forward to nearly the end of the movie. It's the moment when Sean Connery has been shot and he needs the cup of Christ to save him.

Harrison fights through puzzles and near death to find himself on a ledge, hundreds of feet in the air, with the cave on the opposite side, requiring a leap that no human could make. The cup of Christ is on the opposite side, and he can't make the leap as he would surely drop to his death. "YOU MUST BELIEVE, YOU MUST BELIEVE," says his father, and with his hand on his heart, Indiana steps out into fresh air and likely death, only for a pathway to open for him to walk across. MAGIC AND AMAZING. This magic carpet will now become the place for you to RELAX, to calm your MIND from the world's distractions, for you to RECONNECT, for you to meditate and imagine, for you to knock on the door to your soul, and for you to take off on your very own journey of discovery to imagine the world you need, and to manifest what you require to move forward. It awaits you now.

I've Been Automatically Signed up to the World

I know you may think that my last page was crazy, being about magic carpets, but as I sat here writing this book, I turned the page of a magazine I have on my table, and the photograph on the next page was one of a lady walking along some cliff edge, with a rolled up rug in her hand, looking for a spot to sit down to look across a lake. It's time to let your imagination flourish and guide you into a world of manifesting the future that your soul and mind requires for you. Now is all about YOU!! When you were born, if you had been given a choice of pill A or pill B—oh, and had been able to make a choice—your life may have been remarkably interesting indeed.

Imagine if "Pill A" would have been a life of subtle and purposeful control, indoctrination, relying on and only being aware of some of your abilities, and wondering always what your purpose was in life.

Or imagine "Pill "B" making a universal connection with who you truly are and your purpose, being connected to and understanding your many magical powers and capabilities, and having the confidence and power to be you and to spread your divine self throughout the universe, making yourself and others truly cared for and loved. It only required you to believe.

I ask you, would you need to think about this choice for long? Of course not, so why wasn't this choice given to you when you were born? Because other people with a different agenda are controlling the world and don't want you to find your magical self and understand the true power you hold. There is and always has been a global power struggle in the universe, and the power brokers and families of this world have tried to conceal it by hijacking governments and legislation, to keep you hoodwinked and occupied in other ways to prevent you from realising. We are an enslaved people, by only the few, and firstly you must realise this before you can properly take back your true self from the people who chose to kidnap you and place you in bondage. It's time to wake up and realise that governments are no more than puppets for the global demons that enslave you and ensure that you remain NONE THE WISER.

Pill B is your route to thinking free and living life. THINK FREE; LIVE LIFE. There were no pills at the beginning, but the global power brokers needed you enslaved, to not only control you from uprisings but to also do their demonic work, which will result in the reduction of the human race and the restriction of what you are able to do and how you think. Chapter 7 reveals the true purpose of this book, and it's for you to AWAKEN from the shackles of this world, to break free and to seize the power and future you were destined to be given, whilst destroying and putting an end to these global power brokers that have evil intent.

How Do I Learn Quickly?

You need to learn quickly; you need to start to learn and trust your instinctive mindset that was gifted to you. It sits inside you; trust me, it's there. Let me show you. The next time you have a dilemma in your life, a moral dilemma, put yourself to the test; trust me, you won't let yourself down. You can't let yourself down; it's impossible. It's why you were given it. Your instinct, your gut instinct, is a universal guide to help you make decisions, take journeys, and say yes or no to day-to-day things that crop up in your life; it watches as you go through troubled waters and take faithful steps when you doubt yourself at times. These issues crop up every day, so it won't be long before you have the next question, decision, or dilemma to fathom out and make sense of.

The next time you have a difficult decision to make in your life or are pondering a situation and you aren't that sure, then trust in the tools that you were given. You must connect inwards and go to your mental magic carpet, the place where your thoughts settle, and you connect with the invisible and the divine. It's the place where manifesting, travel, and imagination take over, and you connect with who you really are now. All you need to do is to ask yourself for guidance. Ask yourself the question, and you will always, and I mean ALWAYS, find an answer. You may not like the answer, but that is only the brain interfering with the true you and providing an opinion. But that's all it is: an OPINION.

Once you perfect the art of going inside for guidance, you will start to feel more secure and peaceful with life and your pathway in this world. Try this out with little issues and questions, and see how you get on. You will love yourself more when you trust and have faith. You see, you aren't alone on this journey. You have backup; you have a divine central source that always has your back if you only decide to use it. Now don't ever get the impression that you will from now on only have JOY in your life, and that things will always be amazing, 100% always.

There are no mistakes in this world, only apparent ones, because along this journey of human life, you are learning and have experiences to receive, and they may be painful to your human self. It's all a part of the human waking up experience, and you will see this once your new journey truly starts. Both in life and in business, you must have belief and faith. We all need to go for it. We need to DREAM

THE IMPOSSIBLE DREAM!! Because the genuinely exciting thing is that nothing is impossible for you. Anything is possible, but sometimes it's not able to be created. You have to believe that what you want truly exists out there, but you alone may not be able to create it. You may need a team, and you can always create this team and take the journey to the promised land of opportunity and dreams. It's there. Our beliefs may get in the way of this, but our sanctuary of the magic carpet can help remove obstacles, and the imagination can take us there eventually. We then become the person we need to be, to take us on this journey. Just like Indiana Jones needed to become a person who had faith to reach the cup of Christ, so can we, but this won't be our final crusade.

Do My Habits Serve Me Well?

We will never be complete and the finished perfect human being. The truth is that we are perfect now in our own unique way. Picasso, when he painted a masterpiece, said it was never finished. NEVER. Our quest is to learn and experience life. This will include experiencing many types of emotions, both good and bad. Good and bad are just human concepts. All emotions are good because, ultimately, that's how you learn, through experiencing all aspects of a human adventure. Remember, we are spiritual beings having a human experience. Never forget that, ever. We are always changing, whether we like to admit it or not.

"We delight in the beauty of the butterfly, but rarely admit the changes it has gone through to achieve that beauty." – Maya Angelou

Given the choice though, we would all prefer the scenic route to life, but all too often choose a much more painful, drab, and boring route—why? We allow life to get complicated sometimes, so it's best to travel emotionally light and always go inside for emotional guidance on what's right for you. Your life will be richer for it. The seeds that we are planting today in life, won't bear fruit immediately; however, they are sitting there ready to make an appearance for you when the time is right. Have faith, remember!!?

Sometimes you may be given an unexpected detour, which may seem a huge inconvenience, but it's been given to you for a reason. Enjoy, let it enrich you, and you may understand the reason behind it in time. All too often, people I coach have all kinds of excuses for why things don't get done or why things apparently go wrong. STOP MAKING EXCUSES. If you are going to CREATE THE LIFE YOU WANT and take responsibility for the good things, then do it for things that look like they have gone wrong too. It's okay; no one is going to tell you off. You are unique, and not all things will look like they are running perfectly; but trust me, there is a reason behind it, and if you want to reach your goals, you must change those habits.

Habits are the vehicle that gets you there, and sometimes it can be a bumpy journey, but just like the magic carpet, grip tight, hold on, and take the bends, because it will be beneficial in the end … always. All your habits will need reviewing to see if they serve you well, so go grab your journal and start to write some of them down. Again, keep your journal close by at all times, and record those moments when you notice that your habits are serving you well or not so well. We want you to flourish, and this will happen when you establish firm foundations in your life, just like a house. Write everything down; if you don't think it, you can't change it. Once you know what you want in life, you can start to flesh out the job description for the role and the habits you need to develop to be the person you need to be. So, just as an actor will rehearse a role, before it's perfect, you must do the same too, after inventing the character you need to become.

Do I Have the Mindset to Succeed Here?

If you are going to learn to live your best life, then ultimately you will need to change some things, right? Otherwise, you will continue to get the same results you have always received, and that's not progress, is it? Mindset is everything, so if it's not working for you, then believe me, it must change. A small, new habit a day keeps despondency and complacency at bay. This is a journey we are on, and it's not about how quickly we do it. When people embark on a diet, all too often it will last for a short term, because people resort to "type," and we need to alter your type. "Type" is another way of saying the habits you have chosen to adopt. We are only going to change the choice of habits and place exciting new ones in their place, but it's best to only do a few at a time.

Many of my clients will choose FINANCE as an area they need to tackle first and foremost, and little modifications can make a massive difference. Many will say that money is tight and they can't afford to save. This normally means that they are just unwilling to make the changes required to make this new mindset happen, right? Even saving $10 a week can make a difference over the period of a year. We create blockages to change, but once you have fleshed out the person you need to become to achieve your goals, you simply can't let these blockages remain in position. Blockages will be smashed into tiny pieces when you know your goals, the person you need to become, and the essential habits the person must have now. IT'S YOUR ROLE.

Association can be vital in changing mindset. A positive affirmation, a song, a piece of music, a smell, or a location (magic carpet) can associate you and your mindset instantly into the person you need to be to move forwards. I remember a time after my divorce, in my 30s, when I needed to keep a positive mindset. A few demons had crept into my brain and had taken over temporarily. I decided to go on a rampage of having affirmations all over my house: in the kitchen, on the TV, the toilet, the bathroom mirror, the fridge door of course, and on the dashboard of my car. It didn't matter where I looked, there were positive statements for me to read and digest.

It was a little embarrassing when people visited and, to tell the truth, I did cover a few up, but this is YOUR LIFE, and everything is important if it keeps you on your path. I found it so useful because my kitchen affirmations made me drink water and eat healthily. My bathroom mirror notelets told me I looked amazing for my age; the toilet one, to flush, lol. They all had their uses, and they kept me positive, and I grew to love them and to enjoy reading them each day. With sticky notelets, it's always great because you can easily change them or move them around. Later, in my office, I would put large notices and messages on the wall to give me great impact and awareness of what I needed to think about each day, AND IT WORKED. I have used them ever since, and even with books, I scribble all over them, my feelings and little notes, so that I can see how I have progressed in life, and it also allows me to find things easily now in a book.

The next chapter will teach you how to re-invent yourself and show you whether your results match your true potential in life. It's time to focus and change your world forever.

Questions:

- You were born with no instruction manual. You can achieve much more than you could ever imagine. YOU CAN DO AND ACHIEVE ANYTHING. Imagine if you won a prize of 10 million dollars. Write 10 M $$ at the top of a blank page, and I want you to write down everything you would do with that money—where you would live, what you would do each day. How would you live your life? Write it all down, and meditate on the feelings that money and doing those things would give you. Also, in a separate meditation, I want you to imagine you have won that money and your life has been transformed. What does that feel like?

- I want you to purchase a magic carpet, off myself if you fancy. I want you to use your magic carpet three times a week, and write down all your thoughts and feelings. If you have jumped to the questions, then go back to the chapter and read the magic carpet section. It's time to travel.

- Remember that IMAGINATION can take you anywhere. If you relaxed and let your mind wander, where would it take you? What places would you visit? How would you spend your time; what would you look like? What is your imagination naturally drawing you towards? Take note, this is you talking.

- You need to start taking action. Through action, you experience, you grow, you learn, you develop, and you reach your goals. Set a plan to take one action each day. Keep a log of what actions you take, and see what results you get in a few days. Have your favourite affirmations pinned up around your home and work area. It's important to keep focused and to have constant, powerful, visual reminders. Write down in your notes how you feel each day, your thoughts, actions, and all your successes, as well as hiccups along the way. It's all your education. Now decide what improvements, what new focuses and new initiatives and goals, you need to set yourself. Go wild!!

Bonus Real Magic Formula:

Knowledge will take you from A – B, but your imagination can take you anywhere. We struggle to establish what we truly want in life because, so often, we are indoctrinated with a mindset of limitations and complacency. We are taught to settle for a life full of limitations, and we fail to see true opportunities, or we live in fear of change. We disconnect from our passions, and through fear and acquiring responsibilities, we stick to a life that brings us very little satisfaction and contentment. We lose our direction, our life force, and our passion. Life is passing us by at rapid speed, and you need to grab it with both hands and experience everything you truly desire. The magic carpet is a place to go to connect with you and your true passions. Your imagination will connect with its source and unleash an abundance of opportunities, giving you fuel for your soul to start off on your journey. See my magic carpet story and let your soul live once again.

CONNECT WITH THE UNIVERSE
WITH YOUR VERY OWN REAL MAGIC CARPET.

Chapter 8

Change the Way
You Look at Things

8

We All See a View; Do We All Feel the Same About It?

Beauty is in the eye of the beholder, right? We all see things differently, right? So who has got it right in this world? Maybe there just isn't a RIGHT anymore, and maybe there never has been, but we have all been taught that there is a RIGHT and a WRONG. But that's quite divisive, don't you think? And it ensures plenty of pressure all the time to get THINGS RIGHT. The major problem this creates is an unwillingness to try things, for fear of getting it wrong … so let's not try, or I will feel bad.

Getting it right	Feeling great
Getting it wrong	Feeling bad

Instead of the following perhaps –

Trying something new	Feeling wonderful
Learning something valuable from a mistake	Feeling wonderful

We simply set ourselves up for feeling bad in this world all the time, simply by the way we are taught to look at things and the need to always get it right. With a constantly evolving universe and a world that continues to evolve and change, we simply can't learn something once and expect that learning to be relevant and correct as we continue to evolve, can we? Surely, if the universe that we reside in continues to evolve and change, so must we, right? Our bodies and

109

major organs continue to renew themselves; and quite simply, I'm not the same person I was a few years ago.

So learning, true learning in life, must be continuous and in an environment that allows you to try things in order to find out what's best FOR YOU in this world—SURELY? You may try something and not enjoy it, but the answer is to persist and stick with something even though you have it wrong, it makes you feel bad, and it takes up time, preventing you from finding the correct pathway or solution. Unless we can learn through our successes and failures, we will never truly evolve, because the stress to always know the right answer before you explore will kill your soul dead.

All too often, my coaching clients connect their view of life to things that have gone right in their lives, but most often when things go wrong. If we went to London once in our lives, and we got mugged, we would never want to go there again because our perception is that London is full of muggers, and it will cause us pain to return. But maybe you work in London and you have no choice. When you change the way you look at things, the things you look at change. Turn everything upside down in your world and see if your view of the things in your world continue to serve you well or not, including people. If they don't, then change the way you view and feel about them—it's that simple.

My Sights Are Set Far Too Low

Your irresistible offer in life must be connected to your SUCCESS CYCLE, and it's pivotal to see this in the right way if you are going to be true to yourself and your pathway in life. Many coaches consider the Success Cycle in life to consist of the following:

- YOUR POTENTIAL
- TAKING ACTION

- YOUR BELIEFS/CERTAINTY
- YOUR RESULTS

In actual fact, there is much more to your SUCCESS CYCLE than this, and it consists of the following:

- YOUR POTENTIAL – What is it? What can it give you?
- VISUALISATION OF YOUR POTENTIAL RESULTS
- MOTIVATION/INSPIRATION TO ACHIEVE
- TAKE ACTION
- AFFIRMATION/VALIDATION
- BELIEFS/CERTAINTY
- WARNING – SABOTAGE AREA!!
- GIVE YOURSELF AN IRRESSITIBLE OFFER!!

It's vital that you understand your potential in life, and therefore you need to ask your close circle for opinions about what they think you are good at and your personality traits. More importantly, it's necessary for you to go inside and meditate. Meditation will allow you to relax and remember a time when you were free and uninhibited in life, when your dreams were YOUR DREAMS and not influenced by opinion/exam results, money, or opportunity. YOUR DREAMS are exactly that—YOUR DREAMS—and it's not for them to make sense; it's just for them to rise to the surface and be connected back to you and be acknowledged. Write them all down, the crazy and the apparently unobtainable—they all matter and count.

Does YOUR POTENTIAL match YOUR RESULTS?

Why not? The reason is that you have never ever been truly encouraged to explore your true potential, or given the skill set to develop it further. It's all well and good going to school and learning about physics and chemistry, for you to use it only once ever in your life, while you skip over the essential basics of life that will shape your world in your lifetime every day. Crazy, but that's the way it is driven in this world, and you can only suppose its deliberately designed to hold you back in life, and for you to settle for low or minimum goals in life. The truth is that some people are to be the slaves to carry out the dreams of others, so it's important to establish which sector you will fall into, if indeed there must be sectors at all.

> *"Most people are slaves helping out*
> *with other people's dreams."*
> – David Ian Charnock

It's time to climb on board your success cycle and ride to your ultimate freedom, and it starts with knowing your true potential.

Am I Allowed to Reinvent Myself?

The truth is that we are reinventing ourselves every day, but unfortunately not in the way we should be. What you focus on is what you attract, so it's that simple. If you want to have something different in life, then focus on what you want NOW. Once your potential is unveiled and acknowledged by yours truly, then it's time for step 2, and that is to *visualise your potential results.* Again, this is an opportunity to relax in a calm moment and single pointedly focus on each one of your potential opportunities, and let your mind and soul run away with itself in wild abandon.

Imagine what your potential looks and smells like, and what it would be like to reach out and touch it—how does it make you feel? Where could this bucket full of potential take you? Imagine, without limits, what your life could be like if you reached your full potential and beyond. What would your life look like? I want you to visualise what a typical day could look like in your new world of potential. I then want you to remember as much as possible, and take loads of detailed notes in your journal or notebook. I think now is the time to consider using a VISION BOARD; in fact, forget the word "consider"—just DO

IT. You need a vision board because this is going to be where you mix all the ingredients of a wonderful cake you are making, and it will keep you focused at all times.

If you want to know more about vision boards, then simply go on my website and obtain one. You will soon wonder how you lived without one. Simplistically, it is nothing more than a board that you can hang up with all your ideas on it, to always see and to change as you see fit. With your potential thoughts and ideas in mind, I want you to cut out of magazines or download images that you can use for inspiration about your potential, and pin it on your vision board. It will keep you focused and your thoughtful juices always flowing, if it is always in your eyesight. Remember that what you focus on, you attract, so think and focus carefully, lol. Make your vision board attractive; this is your space, it's your world, and it's there to be an inspiration and a focus to you, always.

As you reach a goal, or your potential, then feel free to change your vision board to reflect your achievements ... whoop whoop!! IT'S ALL ABOUT YOU. Remember that in life. This is not a selfish act or thought; it is a fact, and it needs to be upmost in your world. WHY? Well, I will tell you why. Because if you are looking after yourself 100%, and you are achieving and developing your life, then you can be a support and a positive in other people's worlds. When you are the best you can be, then others are inspired to do the same around you. If they are true friends and value you as true friends, they would support you from a need to see you happy and fulfilled. I'm not encouraging you to look down on people or to consider yourself superior to others, but by being the best you can, you can help so many others too.

I hope that makes sense. Selfish, you are not. Focused, YES YOU ARE, from now on, and achieving will take you forward and make you the satisfied and successful person you need to be, in life and in business. It's important to surround yourself with people who will keep you on your path and not distract you or take you from it. Sometimes you have friends and family who will swallow up all your time. Sometimes they swallow up all your energy, and if they swallow up both, then its best that you do something about this quickly and get new friends.

From a Ford to a Ferrari

I've told the story many times in coaching, about how I always wanted a flashy Mercedes sports car, but I was driving around in an old Ford. However, every time I got in that car, I visualised I was in my sports car, and my persona changed instantly, turning me into the truly amazing and successful person I knew I was in life. The next stage is true: motivation/inspiration. If you don't have these in abundance, then your goals, or what you intend to focus on, won't truly attract them, because they just aren't important enough to you. When you are motivated and inspired, then you are an unstoppable force. You need these ingredients.

It's all too common for people to go on diets and join fitness clubs in January after an indulging festive period. But within days of starting a diet or a gym, people are struggling and coming up with reasons not to keep going and following through. It's a challenge that is doomed to defeat from base 1, because there is no sustained motivation or inspiration to reach the goal—no irresistible offer to you whatsoever, no new habits to get you there—so best forget it before you start, people, and save the gym membership and effort. I should just say that not all negative situations are negative, and that goes for people too. Some of the most stupid and negative people have been my most important teachers.

One boss that I had was so insecure and unprofessional, he taught me everything I needed to know about how not to manage people and business. A bully in every sense, he taught me in so many ways how not to do things. He was overly qualified as a teacher of the "how not to do it" school, and for that I commend him for being one of my greatest teachers. If he is reading this book, he will surely know it is him to whom I refer, because his ego will not allow him to miss out on the compliment.

Having the right motivation and inspiration is like having top quality motor fuel in your motor car, but as well as that, you need to have unwavering focus to believe that you will achieve what your potential has said you will achieve. When you are inspired, you fall into sync with the universe. The universe wants you to be inspired, so once you have bought the ticket, you can commence the ride and hold on and trust. Inspiration and motivation get humans moving forward and in sync with everything else. Inspiration and motivation is the magic dust of universal creativity, and once you learn to access and activate at the source, then your life will take a turn for the better, and you will feel at home and content. We have lost most if not all our universal life skills, and re-connecting to the source of the universe gives us access to the toolbox of life, which was ours at the birth of our human existence to use and enjoy. This toolbox was removed by society, and it's your universal given right to have it by your side at all times and to use it and educate yourself on its capabilities. You can't use it up, and you can't wear it out, because it has been passing through the solar system since time began, and your tank will never be empty provided you access it correctly.

I Think, Therefore I Am

"To take action" is next, or should I say to "take affirmative action" by always moving one step at a time forward. So often, we live out our lives in our brains, which reside in a grey splodge inside our craniums. Our brains are creative, and so much hard work is manifested inside our heads, but true EXPERIENCE requires that we take action in our Earth existence lifetime. We need to implement and feel the process by taking action. Before our Earth journey began, we were enjoying a spiritual existence, but to truly experience an experience, you need to place that spirit inside a machine that allows you to do so.

Our body is the machine that allows us the five senses we were given at birth. These were to go alongside the other senses we had perfected whilst we were spirit only. We are really born with six senses though: seeing, hearing, touching, smelling, tasting, and the sixth sense, which is the MIND. Do a search on Google and see how many senses there really are in the human body. I would just like to touch on one area: THE GUT and GUT FEELING. Have you ever experienced a moment when you feel that things are just not as they seem? A moment when you feel you may be in danger yet there is no obvious signs around to confirm such a feeling? What exactly are those moments? What is going on when you feel like that? Are we picking up on some invisible energy or frequency that is conveying a feeling? Are we simply connecting into the numerous other senses given to us by the universe, to be able to equip us for this Earth experience?

We need to be in tune to all the senses available to us. Even with the 5 senses that we commonly know about, we very rarely fully use or stay in tune with what the senses can provide to us by way of information. Just take eating for an example. How often, when eating, do you eat your food and swallow with one mouthful at a time? Savouring the taste, letting the food absorb into your tongue, and really tasting the food? All too often, we are gulping down numerous mouthfuls of food, one after the other or together, and never taste the food at all.

Even our vision is not fully utilised, and we see what we want to see sometimes, instead of what is actually there in front of our eyes. We look but don't really look at all. If you want to hide anything, as Sherlock Holmes said, hide it in clear site, and in most instances, we won't see it. "I couldn't see for looking" is another saying. How can you not see if you are looking? Because we simply don't see, because we train areas that are just mundane or taken for granted, to be out of our vision. This goes for hearing too … how often do you become aware of birdsong, especially when they have been chirping away for quite some time, but we failed to take notice due to distractions and mental overload. What we focus on, we become, and if we are overlooking important areas or blocking out vital messages and communications, then we will be the worse for it. We need to brush the dust off our five senses and study, as well as open, our senses to each one, and then open the door fully to the sixth sense, namely the mind. Don't let the toolbox of goodies that the universe provided you with, get taken away from you or go to waste. You will be all the better for reconnecting to your spirit self.

I'm Choosing My Scripts Carefully

Once we have started to take action, then we need to establish affirmation/validation in our quest. Basically, we need to know that what we are doing with our goals and journey is what we had intended, and that we are utilising our potential and motivation, and are continuing to be inspired. We play so many roles in our lives, and it's important that we now start to play the roles that suit us, and therefore receive the correct scripts. Better still, instead of waiting for the right scripts, let's develop and write them to be tailor-made for ourselves. How would that feel?

Our role/script must validate our journey and what we seek to accomplish. It needs to be the vehicle that takes us to our ultimate destination and gives us the reassurance that we are doing the right thing, and not too many tweaks are required to get us there safely and suitably enthused by it too. We get easily hijacked along our journey sometimes, and are asked or even told to take on a new role or even a previous role we have done in the past. Those days are gone and behind us now. You decide the movie you are going to star in, the leading role you intend to play, and the story line and script ... there, it's simple. You are the star and the director of the movie; it is that simple.

Your script can be as detailed or vague as you wish; however, I suggest your goals need to be specific, but the journey towards achieving them can be slightly vague, ensuring an interesting ride and journey along the way. We don't want to know everything, and ad-libs can be amazing, can't they? We do have moments of weakness, when we dump our goals and paths to head off and rescue others on their journey, but we must return and focus ASAP on our pathways in life. Too many distractions and your goals are just pointless aims that you will never see through to fruition. I can't stress this enough. If you are simply here for the benefit of others, and waiting for their dramas to come crashing into your world, then you are destined for problems.

You will have friends who never get ahead in life and are constantly having problems in life, with their jobs, children, and relationships. You need to ask yourself WHY? Not everyone is on your path in life. You are privileged, and you should celebrate the fact that you have woke up, and now can do something about enjoying the human life that you were always destined to enjoy. If you are going to give away that opportunity, and hand over your universe-given energy to people who will simply waste your time and ground you down, then you need to start this book again before giving yourself a good hard slap. Feel free to slap yourself anyway and get the blood circulating and use your senses, lol.

I'm telling you now ... if you are still reading this book in Chapter 8 ... THIS IS YOUR TIME. It may never come around again in this lifetime. You will ultimately find this knowledge eventually, but why wait any longer; just grab it with both hands and focus.

The next chapter will help you define who you need to become, and help you create a new role for yourself. It will show you why you are your most important asset, and why you need your very own irresistible offer in life.

Questions:

- What things are you scared to try? Fear of failure? Bad results or feelings in the past? Write out a list of things you want to do in life but are either too scared or maybe feel you are unable to succeed at doing. Now read that list; how does that make you feel? Are your fears realistic? What if our parents decided that because we fell over as a baby and struggled to walk, that we JUST CAN'T WALK. Our child can't walk and we just accepted it. How daft would that be? If it matters, we do it. Write a plan to make it happen.

- Does your potential, match your results in life? Write a list of your true potential, what you are capable of, and see if it matches the results you have received in life. Well?

- Take my success cycle and do a spreadsheet with these headings along the top: e.g., Your Potential, Visualisation, Motivation, Take Action, etc. Now I want you to put a plan together that starts by listing out all your potential. List everything that you are capable of, passionate about, talented at, interested in. I then want you to start filling in the other sections as you focus on each ounce of potential in your body. Use it as a workbook to your success, because your true potential contributes to setting true, realistic goals for YOU.

- Time to get a vision board. Google it and get one now or contact me on my website. Use it every day and make it exciting to use, and focus on it showing your dreams and your true potential. If it's not interesting or exciting enough, then you need to change your goals.

- Start to become aware of your senses—taste, touch, smell, etc.—and really use your senses 100%. Use your ears to listen. Really listen to the songbirds and, when you eat, really taste your food. You will be amazed at how much more satisfying and valuable being in the moment with your senses will make you feel. Also, how about your mind as a sixth sense? Gut feeling? Does it come from your gut? What is it? Keep a log of how your senses make you feel, and try to write down why they make you feel that way. The more connected you are with "you," the more you can understand yourself, enjoy life, and become fulfilled in life.

Bonus Real Magic Formula:

Engage with nature and the seasons. Your senses allow you to do this each moment. We choose to let nature pass by unobserved. Take a moment to hear a bird sing, a river ripple and flow, the wind blow through the trees, or to sit and watch a wonderful sunset. Beauty is all around us, and taking a moment to step out of your daily activities to absorb what surrounds you will always cleanse your soul. Get in tune with the seasons and follow nature's way of getting in tune with the flow of the universe. Summer can be a time for full-on activity. Autumn can be a time to pack in all those final opportunities as the days start to change and we slow our lives gently. Winter is a time to take stock of your year; animals hibernate sometimes and sleep till spring. Recharge your batteries in the winter, and reflect on the year you have had, what you have experienced, good and bad, and be grateful for all you have received. Spring is a time for the garden to show signs of life; buds start to appear, and it's our time to come out of our slumber to be ready for summer once again. It's a universal cycle we need to get in tune with and benefit from in our life.

REAL MAGIC FLOWS IN MOTHER NATURE'S WAY.

Chapter 9

Mind Your Own Business

9

Time to Write Your Own Script

When you are certain and you believe, then you are set for success. CERTAINTY/BELIEFS allow you the ingredients to write your own script in the full knowledge that it is going to work. There is no doubt. When I look back at my life, the only true time I have made significant forward movement with my goals is when I have motivation/ inspiration, certainty/belief, and a good coach to fill in the rest. I can't stress the importance of a coach. It even looks great on your CV when you state that you have a performance coach in your personal and business life.

The investment is invaluable, and when you have guidance, support, and accountability, you will become a high achiever. When you have structure, you have progress. Look at your life now. What support structures do you have in place that will move you forward, and not just forward but at an increased speed towards the goals that will change your life? All the top performers have coaches to take them forward and keep them there at their peak, where they need to be always. The only structure an average person has ever received in life is as follows:

Family Circle from Birth – Often a hindrance more than anything else, as you are passed down the traits and beliefs somewhat limiting from your family circle. The family circle has collapsed over the last few decades, with increased poverty and the single-family structure.

Schooling and Education – Lacks stimulation and structure that will allow you to express yourself and become the best you can be in life. Until coaching and personal development are catered for in the syllabus, this system will continue to provide the "slave class" for the next wave of "rich global elite" to rape.

Social Framework – Add up the salaries of your six best friends and average it out. That is the salary you will roughly achieve. Choose your friends wisely.

Work Environment – Get a safe job and work hard at it. I'm not sure a safe job exists anymore, and working more cleverly has to be the focus, not working harder, surely? You really need to get a job and a side hustle. A job pays for your day-to-day bills while you develop your own side hustle empire. Don't put down roots anywhere you won't be staying more than five years, and even then be ready to move at a moment's notice. It's important to develop your contact list. A quality contact list equals a quality life.

You need to build your life from the sub strata upwards, and that needs thought. Things don't happen by accident, so that means you must make them happen. BE NOW the person you NEED and WANT TO BE. The chances are that 99% of the people around you currently are simply wasting your valuable time. YES, 99%, and that includes family members too. Now let me just clarify this before you go bonkers and toss everyone out with the recycling.

YOUR NEW MAIN LIFE: 99.9% of your new life needs to have:

- Focus, structure, and a coach.
- Support frameworks.
- Continuous education.
- New habits/goals.
- Accountability.
- Success and fun.

- Everything in your dreams.

The other 1% is for socalising with unstructured, time-wasting people and issues.

Your Current Life: 99.9 % wasted

- NO STRUCTURE
- NO GOALS
- NO EDUCATION & DEVELOPMENT
- NO ACCOUNTABILITY
- NO SUCCESSES
- LOTS OF TIME & EFFORT ON MEANINGLESS TASKS AND PEOPLE
- FRUSTRATION
- WASTED LIFE & REGRET

It's time for the NEW YOU to appear.

Invest in Me

In the past, I have invested in numerous coaching programs and educational products, some of which have been useful. However, most coaches sell you a basic service package then, with the ultimate aim of selling you more and more bolt-ons afterwards. If you don't see results from the basic package, then NEVER invest more, is my advice. Now this brings me into the next crucial part, which is: WARNING – SABOTAGE AREA!! When things are going well in your business and your life, you can guarantee a red button will be pressed at some stage, and a SABOTAGE WARNING will sound, and most often it will be ignored.

You may think this is a crazy thought. I always asked myself, a guy who has always wanted more and to be happy as well as successful, how I could do anything to damage my chances of achieving my goals.

BUT IT'S TRUE. I think it's something that pops out from childhood. It sits within us and waits until we are on the verge of having some success, and then it pops out and says, "HANG ON A MINUTE; WE CANT HAVE YOU MAKING LOTS OF MONEY AND ENJOYING YOURSELF, CAN WE?" It may be something to do with your parents who have worked hard all of their lives and struggled to pay bills, turning up in your brain and saying, "IT CANT BE THIS EASY; SOMETHING IS WRONG." We all have these demons that don't serve us well, but guess what ... you can write them out of the movie script, guys. It was a script idea that no longer serves you, and it has now been written out for good. SIMPLE. You are an investment from the moment you are born, and you must self-invest in yourself.

> *"You are an investment from the moment of birth.*
> *Don't lose interest."*
> – David Ian Charnock

If you are running a TAXI business, then the most important asset that you have is the car. If you don't look after it with regular servicing, then you may be out of business sooner rather than later. Now you can buy wonderful air fresheners for the taxi, and get your friends all round to look at it and ride in it, telling you how wonderful it looks and smells. But behind the surface, if you don't maintain and look after the car, your business will soon be in trouble big time. We often fail to invest in ourselves because we think we are more capable than we actually are, but there is some truth in this, and it's like a double-edged sword.

We are much more capable of achieving in life than we think, but we need support and structure to achieve. This is not a journey for one person to make alone. We enjoy the journey by our interaction with others. We think we will get round to doing things, but when unstructured and unsupported, we drift off and get distracted by other non-essential time wasting dramas. A coach will get you there quicker, more focused, and happier, but most of all, THEY WILL GET YOU RESULTS by your investment in yourself.

It's Time for My First True Education

I want to talk about the next stage. I want you to imagine that you are a spirit residing in heaven (or your version of heaven), and that your Creator comes to talk to you, with a proposal.

"I want you to visit planet Earth for an undisclosed amount of time. I know you are happy as a spirit in heaven, but I want you to have an Earth experience, and a wonderful one too. You can have all that you want on planet Earth when you visit, but because you are happy here in heaven, I propose to give you an IRRESSISTABLE OFFER to travel down to planet Earth and to have all that you desire to create while you are there. Tell me spirit being, what would be your irresistible offer to yourself whilst on planet Earth?

We all need IRRESSISTABLE OFFERS in our lives, because they PRODUCE RESULTS, and the results that you want out of this life on Earth. All too often, we sell ourselves short and settle for less in life. Who told you it's acceptable to settle for less in this life? Your universal Creator didn't tell you that you had to settle for less at all. All things are on the table, and you can have it all, providing you play the game by the rules. Unfortunately, some people on planet Earth decided to change the rules and play a different game. However, the universe game still exists, and all you have to do is play by its rules NOW.

So now it's time to receive your ultimate education in life, and to create your irresistible offer to yourself. This offer to yourself will ensure that the results you want will always materialise and come knocking at your door. So imagine that you are up in heaven now, chilling out and having a wonderful, blissful time, and you had the offer to visit or return to planet Earth, but you were quite content where you were in heaven. What irresistible offer would get you to move down here and start the journey of an Earth life? It's no good saying NOTHING would motivate you; this is an opportunity to create an amazing, irresistible offer to yourself, and to write down your true goals and aspirations with no fear of ridicule or someone saying that you must be joking, and that you could never achieve this or that in life. Life awaits you, and an irresistible one at that. All you have to do is create the life you desire, and it starts by defining it in your own head and writing it down. You will see it when you believe it, as Dr. Wayne Dyer would say. So write down your goals, dreams, and desires, and then go make them irresistible and so amazing that you simply could not say no to embarking on the journey to create them. Ensure, when you go to bed each evening, that you can't wait to go to sleep in order to wake up for the next day to get on with your irresistible offers to yourself.

Put Yourself First Always

When you put yourself first ALWAYS, you get results. Results are the final part of your SUCCESS CYCLE. The clarity of the previous parts of the cycle already mentioned, determine your RESULTS. When you get the right results, you create an extraordinary life for yourself, your family, and all those around you, a life of meaning, a magnificent life, and a life of joy, happiness, love, passion, success, and fulfilment. This is the ultimate and is a life experienced on your terms. So if your results don't match your potential, then you need to keep redoing the Success Cycle until it does.

What does an extraordinary life look like to you, and how do you give yourself an exciting, irresistible offer to achieve it and keep the motivation and inspiration going until you reach it successfully? Never ever doubt the concept of putting yourself first. When on board an aircraft, they always run through the safety protocol and will say that if the oxygen masks drop from the ceiling, you should always fit the mask to your own face and mouth first, before your child. If you are not in a happy, strong position, then there is no way you can be there to help and assist others. This is your time to indulge, to be greedy if you like. The universe is an abundance of gifts and opportunities, with no chance of running out any time soon. This is the gift we were meant to receive and understand at birth, but we were disconnected from the universal source.

Ask and you shall receive. However, the universe wants you to make effort, show commitment, and always to have faith in the process. You are a spiritual being having a human experience, and to feel the planet Earth and all its splendour, you need to experience your six senses whilst having a human journey, and to feel ALIVE, to experience feelings and emotions, and ultimately learn from the process to caress the soul for always.

When you die, your human journey is at an end; however, you will slip back into the spiritual form, taking with you all that you have learnt and experienced whilst here on Earth. Your real magic returns to strengthen the larger universal pond of all things, and will be all the richer for it until you are asked once again to provide your irresistible offer to return on a new journey. Who knows where you will pop up, and who can tell what experiences you will be part of, but one thing is for sure, you are magic from top to toe, and the creativity is within you at all times. You just needed to know its location and its access code.

I am me to me, and whatever you think I am,
I am to you.

You are who you say you are. You decide things for yourself; that was always the design, but sometimes we get blown off course, and we need to get back on it safely ASAP. You are invited to now return to your true course.

Selfish Sanity

If we all looked after ourselves adequately, there would be TRUE TIME to look after those unfortunate people who need help and guidance. Look at where you would be in life had you known about your magical array of gifts at birth.

MY UNIVERSAL OATH TO YOU FROM THE UNIVERSAL CREATOR:

My universal gift to you
For the time you spend on Earth,
I will provide you with all the tools you will need,
To create your very own irresistible offer to yourself.
Ask, experience, and you will receive total abundance.

This is the gift to you from the universe. It should never be taken for grant or doubted. When you BELIEVE, you RECEIVE. We have been taught to doubt our capability and to put others before ourselves, but where does this get us? I have witnessed many inhumane situations since COVID-19 became an apparent significant pandemic on the earth; however, some of the ways we have dealt with this virus lacks judgement and a human touch. I attended a funeral last week, where Covid restrictions limited it to 30 people inside the crematorium. People remained outside as mourners, simply to attend and be in the vicinity of the deceased and loved ones. The staff at the crematorium, in complying with the Covid restrictions, instigated the measures in a total inhumane manner, by barking instructions to the mourners outside to return to their cars and leave the area.

A Scottish piper, who was hired to pipe the coffin into the chapel, was told abruptly to stop playing before the coffin had even reached the doors to the chapel. The manner in which they spoke with mourners, or should I say barked at them, looked similar to the way the Nazis were reported to have dealt with the Jews as they rounded them up and placed them onto cattle trucks on the way to concentration camps. I feel that this crematorium should hold their heads in shame; and although they have a job to do, the way it is conducted is of paramount importance if you care for the feelings of fellow humans.

Despite complaining to the relevant bodies and authority, no one has given a full explanation or apology for their conduct on this incredibly sad day. We are human, we are people, we have souls, we have feelings, and when those are treated with scant regard, we are bordering on an inhumane and destructive state. We are and should be better than this. We live for better days, and lots will come out in the aftermath of this pandemic, in the way it happened and was dealt with, and those people who took advantage or were inappropriate will need to be brought to account for their actions during this destructive journey that started in the UK in 2020.

Vaccines are being administered throughout the UK and the world. The benefit of them is yet to be fully appreciated or investigated, and a number of side effects are being reported. What I have heard about is vast amounts of companies and individuals cashing in on the pandemic—the protective clothing (PPE), vaccinations, research bodies—all of which needs financing and then paid by governments and, ultimately, you and me. I'm sure that plenty of good has been carried out too, but when vast amounts of $$$$ are involved, then you need to ensure that moneymaking isn't the only motivation.

Firm Foundations, a Business Master Class

In this section, I'm going to give you the Coaching Tips Master Class to having Firm Foundation in Business. This master class is as simple as it is brilliant, and if you bought the book to learn how to create Real Magic in your business, and to manifest your best 24/7, for one reason, this is it. To be successful in business, and by that I mean your business, you first have to get to that point of starting your own side hustle. A side hustle allows you to build your own business part time, building it up slowly while you live your 9 to 5 existence. I'm assuming you have a 9 to 5 job and it's just not doing it for you. Even if it is interesting, it's possibly not going to take you where you need to go in life, so you need to learn skills to establish a side hustle, for you to create another business to build up steadily. In previous sections of this book, I have spoken about putting yourself first, and it can be no further stressed than in business.

When I interview anyone for a vacancy, I expect to see their profile and their persona out on a social media platform, perhaps LinkedIn. If someone is involved and passionate about their subject, they will not only have the knowledge; they will have the knowledge behind the knowledge. Top flyers will know this and have a CV that reflects this, so it's no good just having answers and viewpoints; you need to know the answers and reasoning behind it all too, or at least know where to find it. So my hit list for you in business, to reach the top, is as follows:

- I am taking it as gospel that you are part or fully qualified in your area of speciality.
- People buy from people, so you need an image, a niche, and a personality.
- Amazing communication skills are essential.
- Develop an amazing contact list.
- You need a coach.
- You need to understand your industry and where the money and opportunities are within it.
- You need a profile, a website (basic is okay); you matter.
- You need a unique skill set. What can you offer?
- You need an agent (if appropriate).
- Know your worth.
- Have an Angle, be mobile, have a home office, etc.
- Always have an offer available for clients or employers to consider.

I will go into some of these in more detail in the next chapter. Have another look at them and digest where you are in comparison to where you need to be in this new world. Employers are more demanding now; however, you need to make sure you are at the top of your game with commercial sense and up-to-date business skills. The key is to know your worth, understand customer's needs, stay customer focused and in touch, develop a hot contact list, and then develop a side business that you will love and prosper from as you move forward.

In the final chapter of this book (but not the journey), you will find out why you need an essential business support team to help, and that nobody knows it all. You will learn about the role of mentors and why true life exists outside your comfort zone.

Questions:

- Who do you need to become, and what role do you need to create to develop new habits, achieve your goals, and be ultimately the star of your show and world?

- You are your most important asset. What do you need to change in your life to put yourself first and achieve your dreams?

- Look at your potential lists and your goals, and then for each goal you have, create an irresistible offer for yourself to achieve this, that you simply could not turn down. What are your irresistible offers for your life?

- Do you have the essential support and elements in place to make it big in business? What are you missing? How can you fill the gaps and give yourself every chance of success? What will it take?

Bonus Real Magic Formula:

You are your most important asset, so you must surround yourself with likeminded people that are in tune with your values and aspirations, as well as emotionally supportive scaffolding to keep you upright and focused during challenging moments in life. To keep yourself in a peak state to be able to achieve your goals, use a combination of music, magic stones, and essential oils (smell and taste). Sounds, smells, and significant objects such as magic stones can change your mindset, similar to having a lucky charm. My website will tell you more. (See my website for more information on magic stones.)

YOUR SENSES PROVIDE REAL MAGIC IN YOUR WORLD IF YOU ONLY ACKNOWLEDGE THEM.

Chapter 10

The World Is Enough

10

A Team to Trust

I've said that this amazing journey should not be undertaken alone. You must consider establishing a suitable business support team around you that you trust to look after you and take you to a higher level. Your time is also valuable, and you need to spend it in the right areas and not in areas where someone else can do it better and quite possibly cheaper. It first makes sense to calculate how much your hourly rate is that you charge out at both for your main job and your side hustle.

The biggest shock for you will be working out your hourly rate for your employed job. Once you start calculating at 40 hours a week, etc., and break it down to an hourly rate for maybe 8 hours a day, you will be shocked at how little you earn an hour—unless you are in a highly paid position, but then you must look at the tax situation and establish how much is taken away by the government, directly and indirectly. Once you have calculated your hourly rate for your employed job, you can then establish it for your side hustle. Again, it's valuing your time out accurately in terms of your charges and true time spent providing the service. You may find that your side hustle is much more lucrative than your employed job, and in any case, this would be the direction to go in.

You can then determine which jobs you should get other people to do in your life, and the ones that you should do. I will say it again: Your time is valuable, so if it is more cost effective for you to keep doing your side hustle, making money at a higher rate than someone who can come in, and say cut your trees down for you much cheaper than the true cost to you … get it done by someone else? So other members of your support team that I would advise you to consider, other than a coach, would be as follows:

Ideal Support Team:

- A Coach – Of course.
- Mentors – Find people who have done what you want to do, and copy them. Why reinvent the wheel?
- A Part-Time Secretary or remote assistant – Admin is cheaper than what you can charge out at.
- A Bookkeeper – You need someone to keep and organise your receipts for tax purposes. It is so vital to keep on top of this area and not lose out by failing to claim all your valid expenses.
- Lawyer – They are vital for those tricky times that may arise from time to time.
- Educational Support – You need to keep up to date on your industry or chosen field, and keep learning new things in any case.
- Social Media and IT Consultant – Your laptop and iPhone are the gateway to the world, and you need to maximise the opportunities for global contact, and to protect yourself.
- Partner/Family – This could go way at the top of the list. It's so important to have a supporting spouse in your life and business. Try having a spouse who is unsupportive, and you will soon learn how difficult life and business can be.
- Insurance Agent – It is necessary to insure your business and your services.
- Travel Agent – You need breaks to have time to recharge your batteries. Have a personal travel agent book out holidays and breaks for you.

The list is not exhaustive, but it's what I needed and preferred when I was underway and motoring in my busy personal and business life.

You Don't Know It All

This is true; you don't know it all, but do you need to? Well, if someone knows the answer in your support team or list of contacts, you will be okay, right? Right. That's why a list of useful and up-to-date contacts is so vital when you are busy developing a business and an exciting life at the same time. However, one problem you may come across when you start to be successful, is thinking that you have made it and that you know it all!!! This is when things can start to go wrong and your life and business can start to decline. You will never know it all, and to think you will, is crazy. I think it may even be called arrogance, and although it's okay to have a little of this, you need to keep it under control.

In terms of knowledge, you need to sign up to a long life of learning, and you want to keep this exciting and updated till the day you are no more. When I first started out working, I was young, and older clients and staff members were so closed to new ideas. They would remind me that they had been in the business for 40 years, and what did I know? Secretly, I would think to myself, "Yes, you really mean that you have one year's worth of experience, and it's 39 years old!! Now, said like that, you realise that the worry is that if you stop learning at a particular age, then actually how old is the knowledge you are using and charging for?

When you have the latest knowledge and insight, you can charge top dollar, so remember that when it comes to education. Mentors are also so important, and it's vital that you find a couple to keep a close eye on and learn from. Don't even be scared about approaching these people to find out more from them on how they became successful. Research people in your area, or those who have made it big in your chosen field, and arrange to go and meet them. Tell them how impressed you are with their success; I'm sure they will love and enjoy the flattery, but this will give you an opportunity to see what they did to be a success in life and business.

You may end up having a lifetime friend, someone who you can call upon for advice, or who knows, you may even collaborate on a joint adventure. What do you have to lose? They can only say no, and then you can move on to the next potential mentor on your list. You won't always hear the word YES all the time, so you need to get used to hearing NO, or not hearing back at all most of the time. Rejection is just part of business and life, I'm afraid, and that's why you need to have plenty of options to consider, because a high percentage won't materialise just because of other people's time constraints, etc. Remember that when you approach a successful businessman, he is thinking the same thing as you: Can I really afford to spend the time with this person when my time could be much better spent doing other or better things? It's that simple, so you may need to be inventive when you approach people, and maybe give them an irresistible offer!!

Follow the Dollar, Not the News

This is an interesting topic about following the money, not the news. By the time you hear information on the news, it is far too late. The news is OLD NEWS, not NEW NEWS. By the time the news issues financial information on the latest stocks and shares, it is far too late. All the purchasing and selling has been completed by then, so you must be aware of the news, and treat it as historical data, NOT THE LATEST. Following the money is always the best policy; leave the news to everyone else. Governments give thousands of pounds worth of grants away each year for different initiatives, and it's worth looking at what those initiatives are so that you can investigate and capitalise on them.

If the government is investing money in a sector, then there is an opportunity to get on board and to look at starting a business here. Energy efficiency and sustainability are big areas now, and governments are constantly looking at changing legislation and improving standards; therefore, there could be a chance for you to get involved and set up a consultancy business, for example. Follow the money, not the news. Its old news, yesterday's news, so don't think it's relevant or current, and if you are hearing about initiatives on the daytime news today, most probably the clever ones were on board the day before, so you need to sharpen up and get ahead of the game.

You need to explore who the regulators are in your chosen sector, who makes the legislation, who the big companies and individuals are, and follow them all the time, looking for potential interest in new opportunities or areas of investment. Social media is excellent for following those people you need to follow; start to read between the lines of what is going on. See the bigger picture, what big meetings are going on in the industry, who sets the agenda, and what the goals and aspirations are of some of the big players. You do your homework and you will be ahead of the game; you watch the daily news and you are behind the game, just like all the millions of others.

You need to stand out, and that happens when you step outside of your box, maybe even your comfort zone, and start to act like you are passionate, inspired, and motivated to make it big and have what you want in this world. Remember, opportunity sits just beyond your reach now, but with a little more stretching, you can grasp that opportunity and make it big in your life. Your comfort zone brings you comfort and nothing else. What do you want in life—just comfort, or a slice of the big wide world that sits just beyond your front door? It's there for you, it's yours, it's exciting, and it wants you to come and grab it with both hands.

"Remaining in your comfort zone will only ever bring you comfort
Peek outside a little and grab a handful of abundance
One handful could change your life forever."
– David Ian Charnock

Everything you will do will require effort on your behalf, so unless you are prepared for this, either pop down to the local magic wand shop or buy a lottery ticket, because they are your only other two options. Not grasping and connecting into the magic of the universe is like buying a Ferrari and using a Ford manual handbook (Sorry Ford, but I do love you) to look after and maintain it. You just shouldn't miss this free opportunity and risk fouling up in your life and wasting time.

Hold Yourself Blissfully to Account

So, here's the thing. You have two choices, I believe:

Either you try to reach your goals all on your own and fudge your way through your life, remaining frustrated at the time it's taking, as well as feeling you are battling against the world, OR

YOU CALL ME (or someone like me ... well, I'm unique, so there's no one like me, lol.)

When you have a friend, a supporter, a confident, a coach, a taskmaster, you can blissfully relax, knowing that there is someone alongside you helping you with this journey, keeping you on track, keeping you accountable, and keeping you ahead of the game. We are busy people with busy lives, but busy doing what? For whom?

> *"Most people are busy getting busier.*
> *You need to get busier doing less."*
> – David Ian Charnock

Trust me, if you are busy, you are a fool. Who wants to work flat out and be miserable? That's not what it's all about, people; it's about enjoying yourself on your inspirational, magic-filled journey, using a support team around you to reach your destination.

"Busy fools don't use any tools."
– David Ian Charnock

Do I need to bang this home any further? Not using your free universal gifts is like trying to knock a screw into a wall with a shoe. You have a toolbox of support gifts provided in life, and inside resides a fully charged electric screwdriver, so to speak, lol, but not literally. You must listen, you must trust, and you must have faith in yourself and the universe to deliver all that you seek. Your life is like choosing a book. Choose wisely, my friend, but should you wish to change and select another story, then you have an endless, gigantic library waiting for you to take out another. You have lifelong membership.

"Life is like choosing a book. Remember to choose carefully.
But should you wish for another story in life,
then a gigantic, endless library
is at your fingertips."
– David Ian Charnock

Reward to Investor

When you invest in anything financially, they always tell you that stocks can go up, as well as down, and your investment is at risk. Your investment in life is oh so different. When you invest in life, you connect with inspiration and provide your time and take action. Your investment in life will only ever gain reward, and even at those moments of turbulence and uncertainty, life will deliver a return and provide an experience that will ultimately give you a bumper payday. It's a WIN WIN situation, and it's a cast iron investment that is AAAAAAAAAAAAAAAAAAAAAA+ rated, lol. Your coach will make sure that you review regularly where you are with your goals, to ensure that you are not only on track but that any changes to the plan can also be reviewed as you make progress along your path.

We set goals for ourselves and then create new habits, but once we set off on the journey and start to experience what the path has to offer, then we can sometimes want to review the goal that we had originally set for ourselves. The journey needs to be enjoyed, and when you dance with your partner on a dance floor, your intention is not to go from one side of the dance floor to the other (A to B), but instead to enjoy the dance and the feelings along the journey. Don't put off doing anything; the right day will never arrive, so you need to seize the day and implement your plan of action NOW. All there is, is the NOW; yesterday has gone, and tomorrow may arrive, but until it does, all you know and can feel is the NOW!!

"NOW!!
Never occasionally wait."
– David Ian Charnock

When you have yearly, monthly, weekly, and daily goals that you are inspired and motivated to complete, you will always be encouraged to stay on track with your irresistible offer, and NOW should be always in your mind. Why we are programmed to delay, procrastinate, and create frustration in ourselves, I simply can't understand; but we do, so we must always be aware. The benefit of regular Zoom meetings with your coach is that it keeps you on your toes and is fluid and mobile, because you can converse by phone or laptop wherever you may be in the world. We need to start thinking globally. The world is at our feet, and we are not limited to just our village, county, or country, or even to our continent. This is a global journey and, believe it or not, it will soon be universal in our lifetime— just ask Richard Branson if you doubt this statement.

You Were Never Alone

I want to thank you for being "none the wiser" and joining me on this initial journey, but there is more to come. Chapter 11 is a continuation of our journey, and it awaits you on my website. And my gift for you is that it's FREE—yes, FREE. You see, sometimes things magically happen for a reason, and we have contacted one another through the universe, and we will forever be the better for that connection. But remember, although we have met each other now, you were never alone. You are surrounded by the magic of the universe, and it is a gift given to everyone who wants it and believes it is there for the taking.

If you want gifts from the universe,
then believe in the universe.
Connect to the universe,
and then it will become a lifelong handshake always,
and guaranteed.

Only society considers that you may be alone; the universe never says that to you. If you connect to the universe, you are never alone. The universe wants you to be happy, fulfilled, and to experience life on planet Earth. Society trained you to be "none the wiser," but you are now a little more wise. If you would like to continue our journey together, then my website awaits you, and feel free to pass my book on to a friend as a gift. If you want to carry on our journey, hand in hand, then I'm only an email or a phone call away. The universe will connect us, and I would love to hear from you always. People matter, and until society reflects the true magic of the universe, then my journey will continue. Until our education reflects the true magic of the universe, my quest will never end. Until people wake up to their birthright and dispense with the shackles of our imprisoned society, I will continue my education to the world. Please spread the word. My website awaits you, and I will be there for you if you reach out to contact me.

For bonuses go to ...

Covid has alienated people and isolated people. Covid has shown us how humanity treats each and every one us when faced with problems and dramas. Some people will survive this pandemic but will never be the same again. Some were less fortunate and will never get to see the new world, but we are all one; we are never alone, and comfort needs to be spread throughout until we then get confidence to step out beyond our comfort zone. Only yesterday, I walked into Northampton General Hospital in the UK, and although I had been in this hospital several times before, I was hit by a sadness that will never leave me. It was full of soulless, faceless individuals wearing protective masks, either standing around waiting or walking the drab and dreary corridors, looking for their ward or department.

I felt totally depressed in a building that is supposed to cure the sick and give hope and support. On the surface, it gave none of those things, and I felt deeply not only for the patients but for the staff who had to work there too. This is not the life that I want for us, and I'm sure it isn't yours either. We want a world of joy, hope, love, care, support, freedom, and opportunity, and until that day arrives, I will continue my message.

I hope to talk with you very shortly, always to be the wiser.

Final Questions:

- What business support team do you need in place? What areas are your speciality? Who is cheaper to employ to do certain tasks, leaving you free to build the business?

- Start to develop a good contact list. Set up a client management system on your laptop, and get to know and take notes about your most lucrative and important clients. Which clients are your most important, and what will it take to keep them happy and enjoying the service you provide?

146

- Mentors – Why reinvent the wheel? Who are the people in your chosen field you most need to learn from? Contact them and see if you can learn further from them. Agree to assist them in some way so that both of you can benefit from this unique relationship.

It's time to invest in yourself. By now, you will know more about yourself, your weaknesses and your strengths. Why travel this journey on your own when you can have support from someone like myself? Get in contact, and let's start an amazing journey for you to reach your dreams and have a world we were both meant to enjoy.

Bonus Real Magic Formula:

When you focus on people and communication, you enter a world of opportunity, love, and abundance. My own success has always been to have the ability to connect with people, establish their needs, and to effectively communicate and guide them to their goals. We don't and can't live in isolation from other people. We need people; we are social, loving creatures, and the magic is to reach out to all of humanity and   see what we connect with and what returns. Always reach out and connect with people, but when you receive back, be grateful for everything. The quality of the return you receive, determines whether they will join your circle of friends and zone of influence, or if you may do business with them. We need more human contact and care in this world, and it starts today with you, now. Genuinely ask how someone is now, and enquire further. See what they say when you ask more about how are today.

REAL MAGIC DUST IS SPREAD BY COMMUNICATION AND CONVERSATION; SPRINKLE SOME MAGIC DUST EVERY DAY.

Thank you all. This journey has been truly monumental and emotional so far. It has been so fulfilling, and my quest will go on to help people and change the world. Let's change it together. Join me on my website to continue your quest.

David Ian Charnock, 1966

P.S. Final Word:

This is your moment to take responsibility for yourself and to not simply rely on the establishment or people around you to have your best interests at heart. The world is a rapidly changing place, and COVID-19 has brought about even bigger changes in the way we live our lives. You can't rely on governments to do the right thing for its citizens anymore. Jobs are being lost, industries are crumbling and new ones are developing, cashless societies are more likely, and the shopping centres and high street shops have deteriorated and will take time to bounce back. Countries and governments are in massive debt, and hospitals are struggling to cope with the backlog of operations and consultations required to help with the sick.

You must take control of your own future, and have faith and belief that the universe will listen to you once you have connected to the real magic that exists everywhere. It's also not a journey you want or need to make alone. The best things are shared, and I await your call or email to say hi and to start your new journey along a new road, embracing love, passion, and real magic. You were once "none the wiser," my friend.

Welcome ... Simply the Wiser
RIP all those who truly perished during COVID-19.

BONUS 1:

Chapter 11, SIMPLY THE WISER, awaits you online at
NONETHEWISERBOOK.COM.

Continue the journey and unlock further magic.

BONUS 2:

*GET YOUR LIFE JUMP STARTED
WITH YOUR OWN PERSONAL COACH!!*
UNLOCK YOU AND BECOME YOUR BEST ASSET
– WHY YOU NEED YOUR OWN PERSONAL COACH;
CREATE THE LIFE THAT RESIDES IN YOUR DREAMS.

You can read any number of books, including this one, or listen to
any amazing guru, but to create REAL MAGIC in your life, you need
to unlock your true self and connect with your inner universal
heartbeat, plus take massive, unstoppable, consistent ACTION.
Learn all about real magic coaching, and prepare to unleash the
MAGIC inside you with your very own MAGIC COACH:
Find out who you truly are, what makes you happy,
and what you are destined to do in your life.
Learn how to unlock your Real Magic consistently, stay on track,
and manifest a life you have dreamt about.
Learn how to fast-track your magic, take action,
and begin to create your new life in 10 days.
Find out how to create unbelievable change and give yourself
irresistible offers in all parts of your life.
Unlock the tools that will set you free from the 9–5 rat trap.
Find out how to create your own sustainable economy
and mind your own business.

Create your own path and become the path, so that you never drift
from it again on your divine journey through life.
Learn how to assemble an excellent network and support team.
Find out how to educate yourself for your journey ahead,
to travel light with no need for unwanted baggage.
Live every second, and the days will take care of themselves.
Find out how to ultimately live an exciting, fulfilling,
and amazing life, enriching all those people around you,
including family, friends, and colleagues.

P.S.

You could always win $10M in the lottery, of course,
and your world would be complete, right?
This huge amount of money would blow you away
and make you instantly feel a particular way, wouldn't it?
But what if I told you I could show you a way to make you feel that
way NOW, without the need to buy a lottery ticket or rob a bank?!!

Interested?
You need real magic coaching with me. Contact me now. You can
reach me by going now to my website www.nonethewiserbook.com

Printed in Great Britain
by Amazon

30982827R00093